1980

EMBROIDERING WITH THE LOOM

EMBROIDERING WITH THE LOOM

creative combinations of weaving and stitchery

PENELOPE B. DROOKER

Drawings by Susan Damon Fritz-Herzberg

PHOTOGRAPHS BY
JANE LOUGEE BRYANT, ROBERT M. WILSON, AND DOUGLAS BARR

 VAN NOSTRAND REINHOLD COMPANY
New York Cincinnati Toronto London Melbourne

Printed in the United States of America

Unless otherwise noted, photographs by Jane Lougee Bryant, Robert M. Wilson, and Douglas Barr.

Unless otherwise noted, all weaving and embroidery by Penelope B. Drooker.

Published in 1979 by Van Nostrand Reinhold Company
A division of Litton Educational Publishing, Inc.
135 West 50th Street, New York, NY 10020, U.S.A.

Van Nostrand Reinhold Limited
1410 Birchmount Road
Scarborough, Ontario M1P 2E7, Canada

Van Nostrand Reinhold Australia Pty. Ltd.
17 Queen Street
Mitcham, Victoria 3132, Australia

Van Nostrand Reinhold Company Limited
Molly Millars Lane
Wokingham, Berkshire, England

16 15 14 13 12 11 10 9 8 7 6 5 4 3 2 1

Library of Congress Cataloging in Publication Data

Drooker, Penelope B
  Embroidering with the loom.

  Bibliography: p.
  Includes index.
  1. Embroidery. 2. Hand weaving. I. Title.
TT770.D74   746.1'4   78-17108
ISBN 0-442-22175-4

For my parents, HELEN and JOHN BALLARD

Preface

As AN embroiderer and a weaver, I have become increasingly interested in the relationships and similarities between needlework and weaving. Starting from traditional embroidery stitches and techniques, I sought innovative ways of combining woven and embroidered structures into integrated designs, using each technique to enhance the other. Similar experiments are being carried out by many other weavers and needleworkers around the country, who are coming up with exciting results in both traditional and contemporary applications. In spite of these experiments, it seems to me that most fiber workers are locked into one field, rarely stepping over an imaginary boundary line between the two disciplines. Thus, this book was conceived as an attempt to communicate some of the many ways in which weaving and needlework techniques can be combined to achieve unique effects, as well as to save time and effort.

The book does not attempt to teach either weaving or embroidery, but rather to suggest many different ways of combining them. The techniques involved are quite simple, though the possibilities for original applications and combinations are endless. Any weaver who is not afraid of using a threaded needle can make use of these ideas. Likewise, any embroiderer who knows how to use even a very simple loom will discover many new possibilities.

My hope in setting forth these explorations and discoveries is that weavers and embroiderers will have as much fun with them—and with their own inventions—as I am having.

Acknowledgments

THANKS ARE due to many people, who may or may not be aware that they contributed to this book: to the many members of the Handweavers Guild of America involved in the Certificate of Excellence program, for which my own techniques were originally developed; to members of the New Hampshire Weavers' Guild—especially my workshop students—whose interest and enthusiasm inspired me to organize my explorations into publishable form; to Gene and Ellen Andes, who pushed me into doing something about it; to all those who allowed me to include their work in this book, particularly to Bucky King for generously sharing the fruits of her research and experience; to Susan Herzberg, Bob Wilson, Jane Bryant, and Doug Barr for their patience and skill in producing the illustrations; to Judith Werner for her patient and proficient editing; and to Mike Drooker, whose moral support was no less important than his endless practical assistance in this project.

Contents

CHAPTER 1

Introduction

MOST WEAVERS use embroidery, if at all, only to finish off a piece, on seams and edges, buttonholes, and other fastenings.

Most needleworkers, on the other hand, take their background material as a given, and go on from there. Of course, fabric with special characteristics, such as an even-weave linen, may be sought for a particular project, but this choice of fabric is usually the greatest extent of integration between background and stitchery.

Each craftsman, weaver or embroiderer, may think of the other's techniques as time consuming and intricate. Using the two crafts together, however, can result not only in time-saving and effort-saving techniques, but also in unique designs which cannot be achieved any other way.

At the present time, integrated combinations of weaving and stitchery are most commonly found in nonfunctional decorative or fiber-art pieces. However, the possibilities for combining needle-controlled and loom-controlled techniques in the production of clothing and accessories, furnishings, and other useful items, as well as in purely decorative works of art, are almost endless. This book will touch upon both functional and nonfunctional applications of these techniques, including both traditional and highly imaginative designs. Naturally,

the individual fiber worker can adapt any of the techniques discussed to his or her particular interests, and then go on to invent original combinations.

Though weaving and embroidery are usually thought of and practiced as separate, unrelated techniques, the line between them is in many ways so thin as to be almost invisible. A few examples may serve to illustrate this close relationship.

The Ghiordes knot (Figure 1-1) in weaving is identical in structure to Turkey-work embroidery. One may make a rya or Oriental-style rug by either technique.

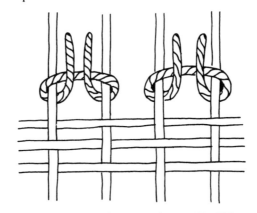

FIGURE *1-1. Ghiordes knot. (Turkey work). This may be woven or embroidered.*

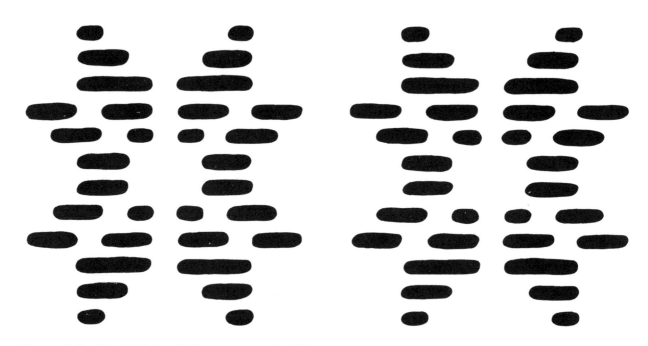

FIGURE 1-2. *Brocade design. Such a pattern may be either woven as supplementary warp or weft or embroidered over a prewoven fabric.*

FIGURE 1-3. *(a) stemstitch; (b) soumak weaving. These are structurally equivalent, but soumak is worked over empty warp threads while stemstitch is embroidered over a woven fabric.*

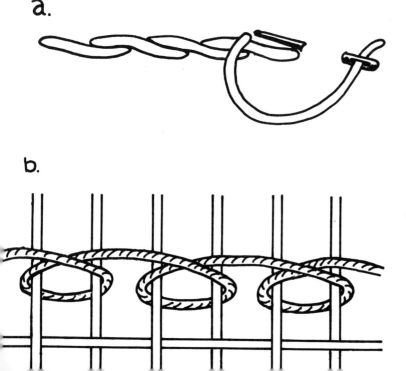

a.

b.

Pattern darning in embroidery may be indistinguishable from brocade weaving (Figure 1-2). In fact, this relationship is acknowledged in traditional terminology, since pattern darning is classified as "mock weaving," while brocade is known as an "embroidery weave."

Other examples of identical structures include soumak weaving and embroidered stemstich (Figure 1-3); Egyptian knot/single soumak and backstitch (the reverse sides of soumak and stemstitch, respectively); twining and woven-band embroidery stitches.

In cases where embroidered work is identical to a woven counterpart, the distinction between the two actually is a temporal one; that is, it depends on whether the knots or pattern threads are added *during* or *after* the weaving of the background material—over empty warp threads or over an interlaced fabric. After the fact, it is sometimes difficult to prove which technique was used in the construction of a given item. For instance, an overshot coverlet could actually be produced by embroidery on a plain weave, although the process would be supremely tedious.

Historically, weaving and embroidery are interrelated in a variety of ways. Many techniques now traditionally assigned either to the loom or to the needle are not only almost identical structurally but also closely related in origin, though their beginnings may be lost in history and any attempt to assign priority to either technique is merely speculation.

Sometimes, however, it is possible to document a precise relationship between a weaving and an embroidery technique. In "Weaving as Related to Embroidery" (see Bibliography), Bucky King summarizes known historical relationships between the two disciplines. Embroidery probably was first employed by our ancestors to decorate skin clothing. As a fiber technique it would have been followed much later by woven fabrics. Almost as soon as weaving began, however, weavers and embroiderers began to swap techniques, often in an effort to save time or more efficiently utilize their tools.

In leno weaving and rya rug-making, techniques that were originally completed entirely on the loom evolved into processes whereby a prewoven backing was fabricated for subsequent embroidery. Each technique involves both loom-controlled woven structures and time-consuming handwork. The evolution of leno weaving into drawn-thread embroidery can be traced back to sixteenth-century Scandinavia. Since weaving was basically a home industry, and it was an exceedingly rare family that owned more than one loom, any way to expedite construction processes and free the loom for other weaving was advantageous. Thus, leno, a woven openwork structure (Figure 1-4), came to be completed off the loom, developing into several types of

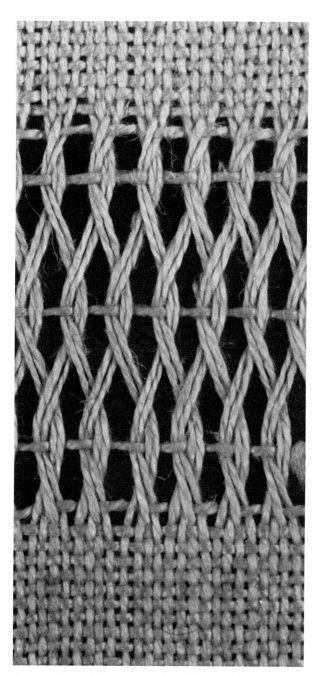

FIGURE 1-4. *Woven leno design. This can be duplicated by embroidery.*

FIGURE 1-5. *Drawn-thread embroidery design. This cannot be duplicated by weaving.*

drawn-thread embroidery that employ much more complex structures than can be fabricated with shuttle alone (Figure 1-5). In rya rug-making, the knotted pile either may be produced on the loom as it was done traditionally, or, if no loom is available, may be embroidered onto a prewoven backing.

Wrapping and needleweaving, used in embroidery, are clearly based on weaving methods. On the other hand, some woven inlay techniques probably originated in the embroidery technique of couching (Figure 1-6), used as early as the twelfth century to fasten metallic threads onto fabric. The Gobelin stitch in canvas embroidery (needlepoint) is used to imitate woven tapestries. Flamepoint bound weaving, however, may have developed in imitation of flamepoint canvas embroidery (Bargello).

There are clearly very close relationships between weaving and needlework, and a wide field of possibilities exists for the craftsman exploring methods of enriching one technique with the other.

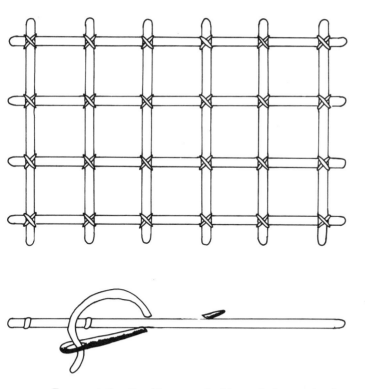

FIGURE 1-6. *Couching, an embroidery technique used to fasten threads onto a fabric surface. Many different embroidery stitches may be used to fix the long floats to the background fabric; only two possibilities are shown here. Woven inlaid threads may achieve similar effects.*

This book describes some of the many ways in which embroidery and background fabric may be integrated during the weaving process. Somewhat arbitrarily, it divides these methods into three categories: embroidery over specially woven background fabrics, embroidery over empty warp or weft threads, and embroidery stitches partially produced by means of the loom.

Embroidery over specially woven background fabrics, discussed in Chapter 3, includes many ways of designing woven backgrounds with specific areas planned for the later addition of embroidery, as, for instance, in the hanging in Figure C-1, the runner in Figure 1-7, and the design in Figure 1-8.

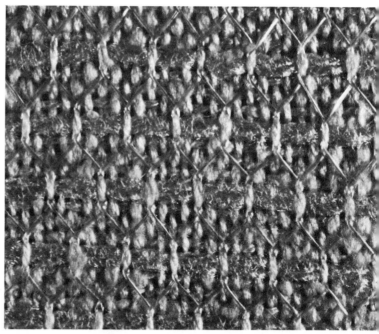

FIGURE 1-7. *Detail of runner by Martha Davenport. Float weave embroidered with herringbone stitch.*

FIGURE 1-8. *Example of embroidered design surrounded and set off by woven border.*

FIGURE *1-9.* Pillow Doll, *by Bucky King. Plain weave combined with wrapped chainstitch and wrapped soumak. Photograph by W. S. King.*

Some of these techniques have been summarized in tabular form, and a brief description of terms and techniques has been given in a Glossary at the end of the book. In a number of cases there has not been room to include a complete description or give illustrations of a technique or embroidery stitch mentioned in the text. However, any reader wishing to explore further will find suggested references in the annotated Bibliography.

FIGURE *1-10. Woven floats as the basis for embroidery stitches: (a) pseudo-running stitch (woven supplementary floats), (b) threaded (laced) running stitch, (c) whipped running stitch, (d) woven supplementary floats, and (e) Holbein-work design with embroidered diagonal lines.*

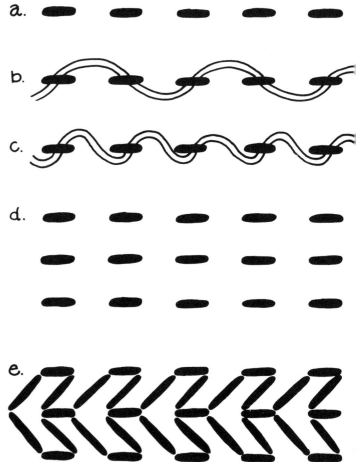

Embroidery over empty warp or weft threads, discussed in Chapter 4, involves traditional embroidery employed essentially as a weaving technique. The stitches are worked over empty warp or weft threads as the weaving progresses, and actually become part of the background fabric (Figure 1-9).

Embroidery stitches that are partially woven, discussed in Chapter 5, make use of the mechanical action of the loom to speed up some of the repetitive aspects of counted-thread embroidery. Many embroidery stitches—all those including vertical or horizontal elements or both—may be produced partially on the loom and then completed with needle and thread (Figures 1-10 and C-2).

Chapter 2

Tools and Materials

MOST OF the items described in the following pages were made on a four-harness loom. Some of the woven structures can be produced on a simple frame loom. Many require only two harnesses and all of them can be accomplished with four, though additional harnesses allow for more intricate designs, additional possibilities in combining techniques, and greater utilization of the mechanical aspects of the loom to speed the production process.

Throughout the book, drafts are given for rising-shed looms, as these are probably the commonest type used in this country today. "P" is used to symbolize "pattern thread" and "B" to symbolize "background thread" where such are used. Otherwise, vertical lines are used to indicate treadling order, numbers representing each harness to define the threading sequence, and dots to show tie-up. In draw-down, or weave structure diagrams, blacked-in squares represent warp threads unless otherwise noted. Usually two repeats are given for generalized pattern drafts.

For some of the weaving techniques in which two separate sets of warp threads are used, a second warp beam is helpful. A perfectly satisfactory substitute can be made, however, by winding warp threads onto a slat or dowel, securing them by fastening a second slat to the first, and weighting this all down with books, washers, cones of yarn, harness weights, or other handy objects. Tension can be controlled by judicious choice of weights. In *Supplementary Warp Patterning* (see Bibliography), Harriet Tidball discusses various methods for constructing the equivalent of a second warp beam.

Another handy item, scorned by many weavers as being a "crutch," is a temple (Figure 2-1). Its main purpose here, in addition to keeping selvedges even, is as a stretcher when embroidery is done on the loom. Together with loom-controlled warp tension, a temple can serve the same purpose as an embroidery hoop, keeping the fabric taut for embroidery, as well as preventing pulled-in edges in techniques where warp and weft threads are distorted from the original fabric structure.

Pickup sticks with bevelled edges are useful for double-weave and block-weave pickup patterns, but a ruler or yardstick will achieve the same result. Such sticks can also be used to hold the size of a section of unwoven warp threads earmarked for later embroidery.

A blunt, large-eyed tapestry needle is the most appropriate tool for the embroidery techniques discussed in this book, as the stitchery is designed to be worked *around* the threads of the background material; that is, through the holes between threads.

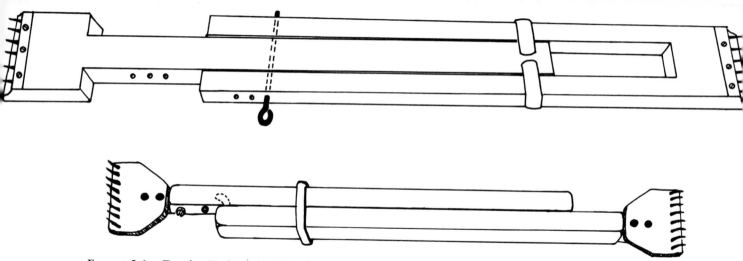

FIGURE 2-1. *Temples. Used to hold fabric selvedges equidistant as weaving progresses.*

With a sharp needle it is hard to avoid splitting threads. In order to make a hole in the fabric large enough to easily accommodate the embroidery thread, the needle should have a similar diameter to the thread. A collection of several sizes of needles is handy.

A good general rule to follow in weaving fabric that will be embroidered is to keep both threads and pattern simple, in order not to compete with the stitchery. Novelty yarns and fuzzy yarns like mohair might obscure or detract from an embroidered design. The same holds true for intricate pattern weaves. Of course, rules are made to be broken, but in doing so, one should give careful consideration to the desired end effect. The relationships between the fabric fiber content and construction, on the one hand, and the embroidery design and placement, on the other, should also be considered.

For samplers, a linen background, traditional for many embroidery techniques, is ideal, giving a strong, firm surface on which to work. A yarn size of about 20/2 or 10/1, sett at 20 ends per inch (epi), results in a medium-coarse fabric that is easy to utilize for most techniques. Wet-spun plied yarns are relatively slippery compared to dry-spun singles of the same weight. Wet-spun plied yarns are

stronger and easier to weave, with less stretching, breakage, and sticking among warp threads, but dry-spun singles may be preferred for use with pulled-thread or drawn-thread embroidery, where selected threads are distorted from the woven web. A fabric constructed of a slightly hairy yarn will hold its shape better around the distorted area.

Any thread appropriate to the stitch can be used for embroidery on samplers. Heavy, soft threads will stand out, whereas threads similar to the background will blend in. Thus, needlework techniques which produce holes in the background fabric for a textured effect are often worked with a thread identical to that used in the fabric. If the intent is to cover the background material completely with embroidery, a thick, soft thread is a good choice.

Either untwisting or kinking in embroidery threads may cause problems. If the motion of the embroidery stitch is opposite to the ply or twist of the yarn, a gradual loosening will occur. Single-ply yarns, particularly, will become very weak if untwisted, and they may break. In the case of linen thread, which is difficult to penetrate completely with dye, the unplied or untwisted yarn may appear lighter where its center is revealed. Of course, if the motion of the embroidery stitch coincides with the direction of ply or twist, the opposite effect will occur and the yarn will become kinky. Either state of affairs is easy to correct simply by twisting the thread back to its original structure whenever it becomes either kinky or untwisted.

Whenever it is feasible, I like to finish up embroidery while the piece is still on the loom—indeed, as it is being woven. The loom acts as an embroidery hoop, stretching the fabric taut, so that both my hands can be used, if necessary, for the needlework. This also allows for some experimentation in stitch size and placement, as well as in overall pattern design, as I go along.

However, there may be good reasons for completing embroidery off the loom, as when the loom is needed very quickly for another project. The major considerations, however, usually relate to the finishing processes (washing, pressing, etc.) which the fabric will undergo.

Since different fibers usually shrink differentially, it is risky to wash an item that has been woven in one fiber (say, linen) and embroidered with another (say, cotton). Even the same fiber processed in different ways, for instance, mercerized and unmercerized cotton, may cause problems.

Weaving and embroidery threads for practical items should, obviously, be appropriate to the intended use. If the item will need frequent cleaning, such as garments or table linens, or if the fabric will require washing or other finishing processes, such as in the case of woolens or linens, the embroidery thread should be of the same material as the fabric thread—wool on wool, linen on linen, etc.

If mixed fibers must be used, be sure to make good-sized samples and subject them to the same finishing processes as will be used on the completed item.

Washing and pressing generally flatten out an embroidered pattern. If a more three-dimensional effect is desired, embroidery should be completed after fabric processing, even if weaving and embroidery threads are exactly the same.

Some embroidery materials, such as metallic threads, either should not be washed or ironed at all or must be washed and ironed at much lower temperatures than background fibers. These should definitely be added after the finishing processes for the fabric have been completed.

In the case of nonutilitarian items such as wall hangings, however, where finishing may consist of only a light steam-press, if that, it may well be feasible to complete stitchery on the loom even if a variety of fibers is included in the piece.

Total weight of materials should be considered since the background must be able to support the embroidery. Large areas of embroidery in a heavy thread may pull or distort an article. (Of course, distortion may be the desired effect in certain instances.) In many items such problems may be compensated or corrected by use of a lining.

It goes almost without saying that soft, thin threads and lightweight weaves are appropriate to delicate embroidery, including work where the woven structure is distorted to achieve a lacy effect, as, for instance, in pulled-thread embroidery. Heavy yarns and tightly woven fabrics are more appropriate for surface embroidery. These considerations will be further elaborated in the descriptions of specific woven patterns and embroidery techniques that follow.

CHAPTER 3

Embroidery over Specially Woven Background Fabrics

THE MOST important rule in selecting woven backgrounds for embroidery is to choose a fabric structure that will enhance the stitchery. For this reason, traditional background fabrics are relatively simple, including plain weave, basket weave, canvas weave, and huckaback, among others.

The handweaver may use these traditional woven structures alone or in combination with other weaves. Unusual fibers may be employed, such as wool yarn for a huckabuck, or a scale of weaving may be used that is different from what is available in commercial fabrics, such as a gigantic canvas weave for large-scale needlepoint embroidery. Background fabrics that are not normally available to the embroiderer, such as double cloth (which may be embroidered on one or both surfaces), are literally at the handweaver's fingertips. When a background material is planned from the beginning to include embroidered motifs, various embellishments can be woven into the fabric, designed to enhance or harmonize with the needlework. For instance, colored stripes or woven pattern areas can enclose or include areas to be embroidered. Pick-and-pick, soumak, inlay, and other weaving techniques can be used for this purpose.

Plain Weave with Specially Woven Borders for Embroidered Motifs

The simplest and the most versatile weave for embroidery, plain weave ranges from balanced tabby to rya rug backing, from weft-faced tapestry to warp-faced narrow bands. Its infinite variety of appearances arises from variations in warp or weft spacing or both, as well as from yarn composition, size, and color. Many of these variations can be planned as foils for embroidered motifs, as can combinations of plain weave with other woven structures.

Perhaps the most obvious method of customizing a plain-weave fabric designed specifically for stitchery is to devise woven borders to enclose or include the embroidered area. In most cases, the base fabric will be a balanced tabby, which is ideal for most embroidery techniques using stitches worked over a specific number of threads (counted-thread work).

Methods for weaving such borders or frames include, among many others, plain weave, twill designs, inlaid supplementary threads, and soumak, twining, and chaining. Plain weave can be used to create colored stripes or plaids (balanced plain

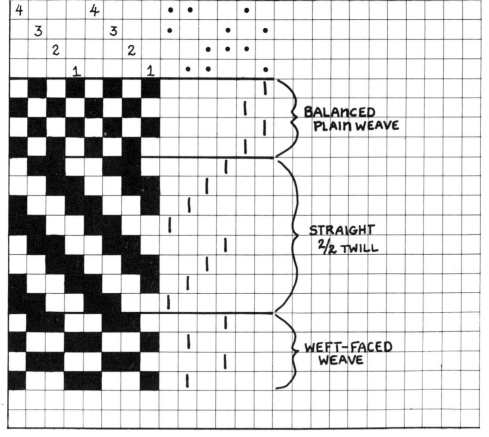

						•	•			•						
4			4						•							
	3			3		•			•	•						
		2			2			•	•	•						
			1		1	•	•			•						

BALANCED
PLAIN WEAVE

STRAIGHT
2/2 TWILL

WEFT–FACED
WEAVE

FIGURE 3-1. *Straight twill draft, with some treadling varia-tions.*

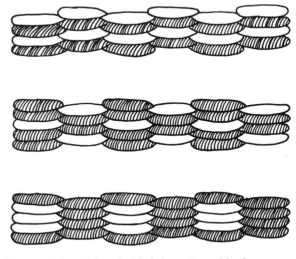

weave), shadow plaids, or warp-faced or weft-faced sections in a single color, in pick-and-pick designs, or in tapestry weave. Inlaid supplementary threads can be put in on tabby, on pattern treadlings such as twill, block weaves (overshot, monk's belt, summer and winter, and crackle), or in weaver-controlled designs.

The straight twill threading given in Figure 3-1 can be used to produce tabby, twill designs, or a weft-faced effect. The latter can be used in a single color or with alternating contrasting colors to form pick-and-pick designs (Figure 3-2). Plain weave, of course, is a two-harness weave and can be woven on the simplest of looms.

FIGURE 3-2. *Pick-and-pick designs. Formed by the sequence in which colors are inserted into a weft-faced or warp-faced plain weave.*

Examples of embroidered designs on plain weave set off by single-color stripes, pick-and-pick patterns, twill, and soumak can be seen in Figures 3-3 and 4-3. A major consideration in devising such woven borders is to achieve integrated designs, with weaving and needlework complementary to each other. Because of this integration, it is often hard to see where the woven pattern stops and the embroidered one begins.

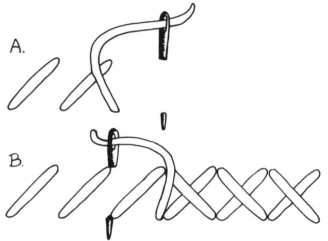

FIGURE 3-4. (a) Tentstitch; (b) Cross stitch.

FIGURE 3-5. Eyelets. Appearance will differ depending on how tightly embroidery thread is pulled.

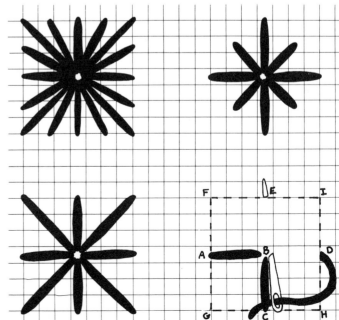

FIGURE 3-3. Sampler of embroidery on balanced plain weave, with counted-thread designs set off by woven borders. From top: Canvas embroidery in tentstitch with weft-faced plain-weave border; Holbein-work embroidery in double running stitch with border in supplementary weft floats over two threads (connected by vertical embroidered stitches to form crenellations); pulled-thread embroidery in eyelet stitch; Assisi-work embroidery in cross stitch and double running stitch with pick-and-pick border; Crewel embroidery in stemstitch, buttonhole stitch, needle-weaving, bullion stitch, French knots, and whipped and woven webs with soumak border.

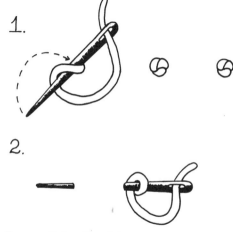

1.

2.

FIGURE 3-6. *French knot.*

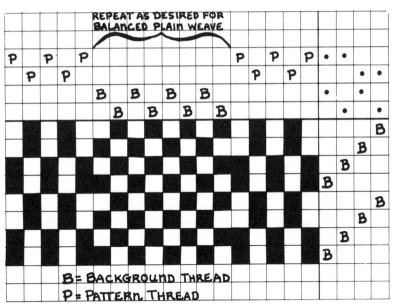

REPEAT AS DESIRED FOR BALANCED PLAIN WEAVE																
P		P		P						P		P		P	•	•
	P		P								P		P			•	•
				B		B		B		B					•		•
					B		B		B		B			•			•

B = BACKGROUND THREAD
P = PATTERN THREAD

FIGURE 3-7. *Threading for warp-faced border stripes surrounding balanced plain weave. Border threads are sleyed close together.*

It should be noted that in many cases such borders can be set up on the loom to run warp-wise as well as weft-wise. For instance, to duplicate the woven border used in the topmost design in Figure 3-3, a draft such as given in Figure 3-7 could be used. Border pattern threads would be sleyed closer together than background tabby threads.

Shadow plaids are block designs woven into a tabby by creating a pattern of either differently-sleyed yarns (Figure 3-8) or of yarns of different sizes (Figure 3-9), rather than different colors as in a conventional plaid. Shadow plaids provide a simple, direct method for weaving a firmer framework around a more delicate fabric.

FIGURE 3-9. *Window screen woven in shadow plaid (10/1 and 10/2 linen) and stitched as a sampler of pulled-thread embroidery.*

FIGURE 3-8. *Pattern formed by differently spaced warp and weft threads, creating a type of shadow plaid.*

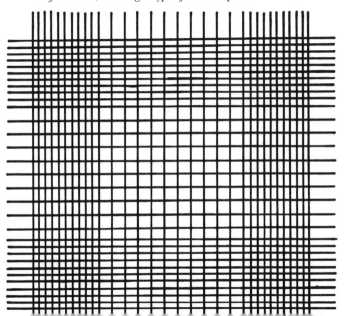

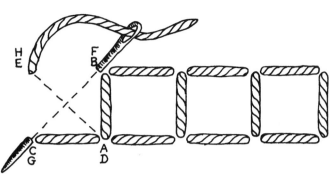

FIGURE 3-12. Four-sided stitch. This must be pulled very tight.

FIGURE 3-10. Details of window screen. (a) Design using satinstitch; (b) Clockwise from top left: designs using satinstitch and four-sided stitch, backstitch (reverse side of stem stitch), and double backstitch in two variations (see Figure 3-23).

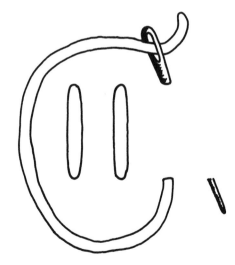

FIGURE 3-11. Satinstitch (in canvas embroidery, called Gobelin stitch). Stitches usually worked close together.

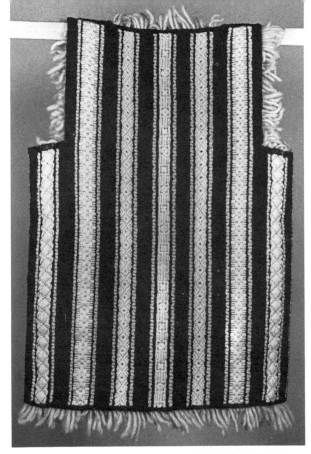

FIGURES *3-13 a and b.   Front and back of pile-lined vest. Weft-faced weave, Ghiordes knots, and canvas embroidery over balanced plain weave.*

Particularly effective on a thin, widely spaced background fabric such as may be used in a shadow plaid is the embroidery technique of pulled-threadwork, in which warp and weft are distorted by pulling the embroidery stitch very tightly (Figures 3-9 and 3-10 a and b). Pulled-thread embroidery may hold special interest for weavers, as it can be used to produce textures impossible with weaving alone.

A warp-faced or weft-faced strip can also be used to provide a firm framework surrounding an area designated for embroidery. For example, the jacket illustrated in Figures 3-13 a and b combines stripes of weft-faced weave, rows of Ghiordes knots, and

stripes of balanced tabby over which canvaswork designs have been embroidered. As can be seen from the layout (Figure 3-14), the vest was woven sideways, to the desired shape, with all knotting and embroidery completed on the loom. The warp was a relatively widely spaced (12 epi) thin (10/1) linen set up on a twill threading. Weft-faced portions were woven in wool, while portions intended for embroidery were woven with the same linen as the warp, in a balanced tabby (Figure 3-15). Needlepoint wool was used in the stitchery. The knots, also of wool, were tied upside down over six ends. The relatively light materials allow the garment to be comfortable though bulky, and the vertical

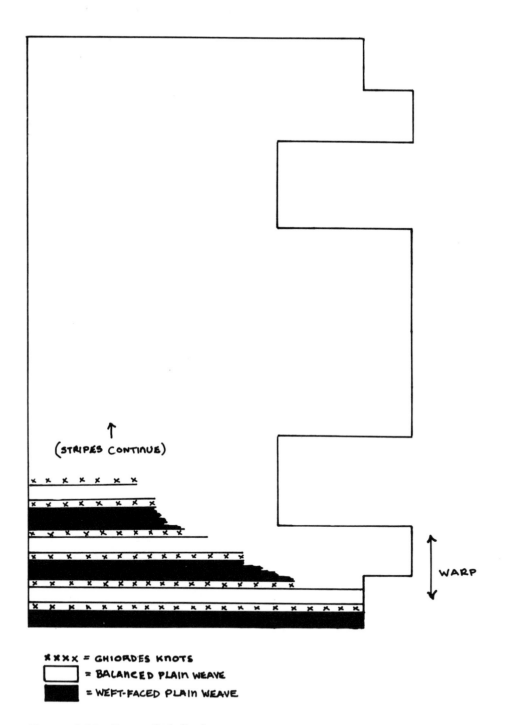

(STRIPES CONTINUE)

x x x x = GHIORDES KNOTS

= BALANCED PLAIN WEAVE

= WEFT-FACED PLAIN WEAVE

WARP

FIGURE 3-14. *Layout of pile-lined vest.*

FIGURE 3-15. *Sample showing construction of pile-lined vest.*

stripes counteract the relative stiffness of the woven material. The embroidery stitches, primarily eyelet and satin stitch, and patterns were chosen for their textural value, as well as for their dissimilarity to woven designs. Multicolored embroidered designs were considered and rejected as being too similar to woven tapestries or bound-weave patterns. Construction of this garment tied up my loom for several weeks. If this had been inconvenient, I could have completed the embroidery off the loom.

Weft-faced plain weave can be combined with canvas embroidery very effectively for flat rugs. For instance, border stripes at each end can be embroidered in an intricate design, while the bulk of the rug is woven. Considering that many needlepointers spend thousands of hours embroidering entire rugs, such a compromise seems to include the best of both worlds.

FIGURE 3-16. *Inlay on same shed as background tabby. (Inlaid thread is a weaver-controlled supplementary weft thread).*

FIGURE 3-17. *Inlay/overlay sampler. Supplementary weft patterns on a twill threading are woven on plain-weave background.*

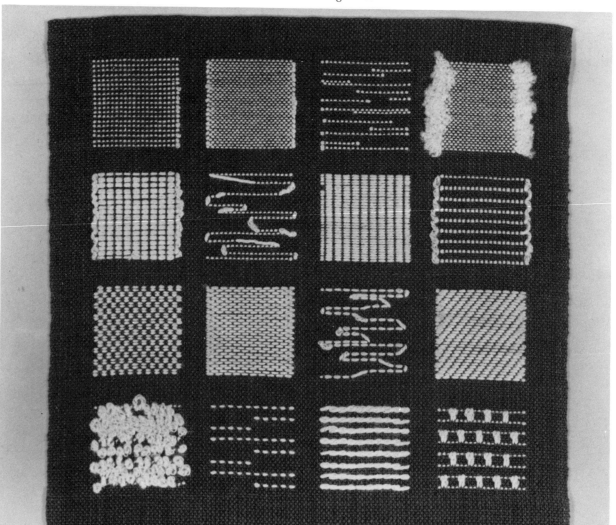

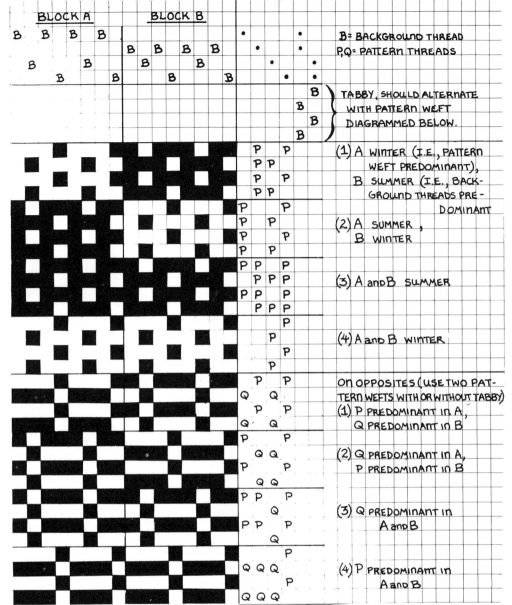

BLOCK A | BLOCK B

B = BACKGROUND THREAD
P, Q = PATTERN THREADS

TABBY, SHOULD ALTERNATE WITH PATTERN WEFT DIAGRAMMED BELOW.

(1) A WINTER (I.E., PATTERN WEFT PREDOMINANT), B SUMMER (I.E., BACKGROUND THREADS PREDOMINANT

(2) A SUMMER, B WINTER

(3) A and B SUMMER

(4) A and B WINTER

ON OPPOSITES (USE TWO PATTERN WEFTS WITH OR WITHOUT TABBY)
(1) P PREDOMINANT IN A, Q PREDOMINANT IN B

(2) Q PREDOMINANT IN A, P PREDOMINANT IN B

(3) Q PREDOMINANT IN A and B

(4) P PREDOMINANT IN A and B

FIGURE 3-18. *Draft for summer-and-winter weave, including several different treadling possibilities.*

To set off shaped motifs, rather than long borders, colored threads can be laid in to enclose or cover a smaller area (Figure 3-16). The sampler in Figure 3-17 shows a variety of inlaid structures that can be woven on a twill threading. Any one of these structures could form an effective outline for an embroidered motif. Inlay can also be used in other loom-controlled pattern sheds, as, for instance, in combination with a block weave, to form a frame for an embroidered design.

Summer and winter is a block weave which can be woven to produce contrasting light (summer) and dark (winter) pattern areas. Essentially, the winter structure is an overlaid supplementary weft on a tabby background and the summer structure is an underlaid supplementary weft. Many possible

FIGURE 3-20. *Woven frame surrounding embroidered design. Canvas embroidery (Florentine stitch) over balanced plain weave, surrounded by a summer-and-winter pattern treadled on opposites.*

FIGURE 3-19. *Inlaid design, in loom-controlled block weave combined with pickup. Summer-and-winter weave and plain weave with discontinuous pattern weft.*

FIGURE 3-21. *Florentine stitch. (Compare with satinstitch, Figure 3-11.)*

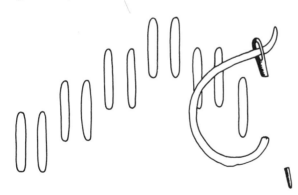

treadling variations (Figure 3-18) make this a useful, versatile weave. Loom-controlled block patterns can be combined with pickup for more intricate designs. Another way to vary summer-and-winter designs is to use discontinuous pattern wefts, as was done for the sample in Figure 3-19. This design includes areas of plain weave suitable for the addition of embroidery. Figure 3-20 is a sample of summer and winter woven on opposites, expressly designed to leave a central section of plain, fairly widely spaced tabby as a background for canvas embroidery.

Any block weave that uses a tabby foundation can

be employed as the basis for such a frame. Crackle or overshot (especially monk's belt) are possible threadings. However, care should be taken to balance the woven and embroidered patterns so that their combination is not confusing. Either the woven or the embroidered pattern usually should dominate.

Plain Weave with Inlaid Designs

In the previous section, we have seen examples of various weaves, including a number of inlaid structures, used to set off embroidered designs worked over plain weave. In all cases, the woven border or frame was subordinate to the needlework. In contrast to that are designs in which embroidery and weaving are equally important, and some in which only a very small amount of stitchery appears.

The laid-in patterns in Figure C-3 are typical of stylized folk designs employed by weavers and embroiderers in many cultures. Such patterns can be either woven (usually in a weaver-controlled pick-up shed) or embroidered on a plain-weave fabric. Unless the loom is used to control pattern threads, as is sometimes true for simple designs, neither method is speedier than the other, and the choice of one over the other would be largely a matter of preference or tradition. Embroidery is often used for small, isolated motifs, whereas long border designs may more frequently be woven, though it is difficult to generalize.

It is possible, of course, to combine a loom-controlled laid-in pattern with embroidery to gain greater design versatility without sacrificing speed. The border design in Figure C-4, essentially a laid-in design over a tabby background, was woven on an overshot pattern threading. To create a graceful transition between pattern and plain weave, the scalloped detail at the top of the border was stitched in with needle and thread.

Besides its use in traditional geometric patterns, the inlay technique is very effective in creating tapestry-like designs. Stitchery can be used with such designs either to add additional texture or to delineate portions of the design that would be difficult to weave, as in Figure C-5. Here, a very small amount of embroidery—in the sun's rays—completes an inlaid design.

Half tapestry is a specialized type of inlay on a plain-weave background. A Swedish technique, it utilizes a relatively widely spaced background tabby together with a weaver-controlled inlaid supplementary pattern weft to create either opaque designs on a translucent background or translucent designs on an opaque background (Figure 3-22).

FIGURE 3-22. *Half-tapestry weave sample. A 14/1 linen tabby with 10/2 linen inlay, 12 epi, was used.*

Because of the combination of opaque and translucent areas thus created, the technique is sometimes called "transparent weave." Only two harnesses are required for this weave. As it is basically a weaver-controlled structure, great versatility in design can be achieved.

In half tapestry, linen is ideal for warp and tabby weft. If it is hairy it will hold its shape well in the plain tabby areas. A yarn just heavy enough to fit between each tabby pick without distorting it should be chosen for the supplementary weft. Linen, cotton, and wool all work well. The supplementary weft is inserted after each tabby pick, either in the same shed or on pattern. Patterns may be laid out on graph paper, or designed spontaneously as the weaving progresses. When weaving a preplanned design, take care to square the tabby by eye, or the design may be distorted.

Embroidery can be used with half tapestry, as with other types of inlay weaving, both to add design elements that might be difficult to weave and to create textures in contrast to the rather flat, smooth woven surface. Both of these purposes are served by the small amount of embroidery added to the central portions of the flowers in Figure C-6, as well as by the French knots used for the leafy areas of the tree in Figure C-7.

Shadow work is a type of embroidery that combines well with half tapestry, particularly in pieces designed to be back-lit, for instance, used as lamp shades or hung in windows. This embroidery technique uses double backstitch (Figure 3-23) which looks quite different depending on whether it is back-lit or front-lit (Figure 3-24 a and b). In India and elsewhere, double backstitch is worked on fine, translucent cotton in floral and paisley-like designs. It is a versatile stitch which can be used to outline or fill an area of almost any shape, as long as it is not so wide that the threads across it become impractically long.

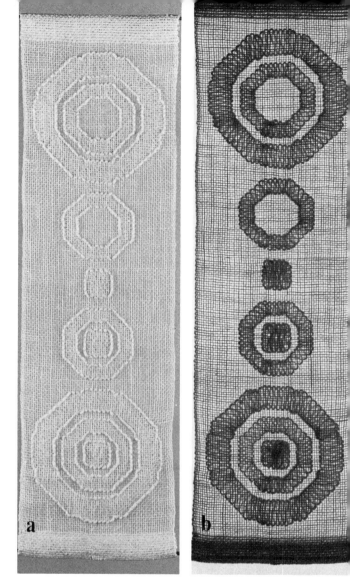

FIGURE 3-24 a and b. Front-lit and back-lit hanging. Double backstitch over widely spaced tabby.

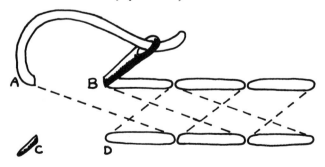

FIGURE 3-23. Double backstitch.

26

Pulled-threadwork is another type of embroidery that combines ideally with half tapestry. The textures created by distortion of warp and weft threads from their original perpendicular relationship contrast well with both opaque and translucent areas of conventional half tapestry.

Figures 3-25 and 3-27 show small designs in which the translucent tabby areas of the woven design have been completely disguised by pulled-thread embroidery. Needlework was done with the same thin linen thread used for warp and tabby weft. Thus, the stitches blend into the background threads and the holes, or negative spaces, are allowed to become the dominant feature of the designs.

FIGURE 3-25. *Hanging. Half tapestry with pulled-thread embroidery over translucent portion. Diagonal raised-band stitch with outline in satinstitch.*

FIGURE 3-27. *Hanging. Half tapestry with pulled-thread embroidery over translucent portions. Eyelets and satinstitch.*

FIGURE 3-26. *Diagonal raised-band stitch. This must be pulled tight for proper effect.*

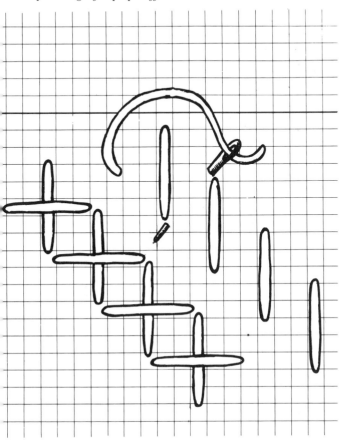

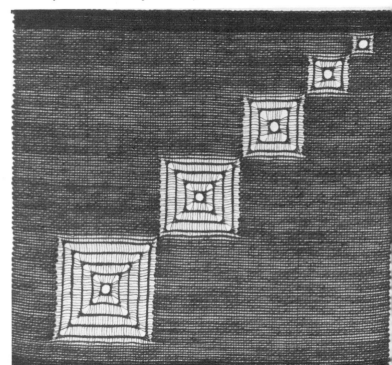

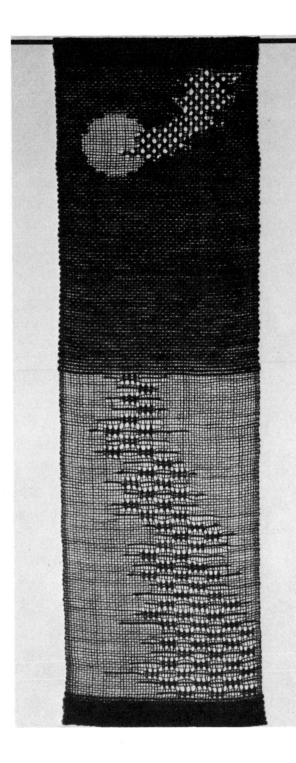

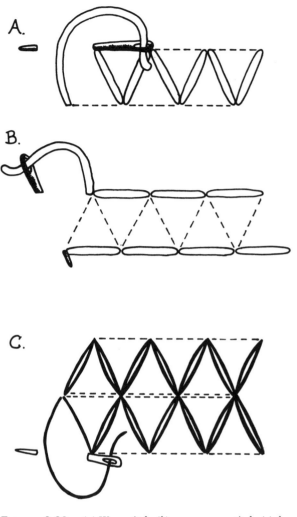

FIGURE 3-29. (a) Wavestitch; (b) reverse wavestitch; (c) double wavestitch (two rows).

FIGURE 3-28. Hanging. Half tapestry with pulled-thread embroidery. Double wavestitch and thicket stitch (made up of satinstitch and double backstitch)

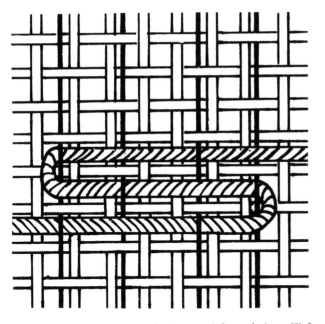

FIGURE 3-30. *Structure of Moorman inlay technique. Weft pattern threads are held down by thin supplementary warp threads which may be almost invisible. (Compare with inlay on tabby, Figure 3-16).*

In Figure 3-28, pulled-thread stitches are used more sparingly. Note that, to minimize distortion of the selvedges, a stitch that pulls together weft threads but not warp threads was chosen for the bottom part of the design. (Compare with the window screen in Figure 3-9, where selvedges were pulled in significantly by the embroidery.)

An additional design possibility for half tapestry combined with pulled-thread embroidery is the use of a large-scale background tabby, very widely spaced (say, 10/2 linen at 4–6 epi). Such a structure does not hold its shape well by itself; it is only barely practical for half tapestry if a design is chosen in which the plain tabby areas are very small. However, the tabby areas can be stabilized and held in place if they are completely covered by pulled-thread embroidery, as in Figure 3-25. This can be a relatively quick way of producing a large woven piece with interesting textural qualities.

Moorman technique, an inlay weave developed by Theo Moorman, is not, strictly speaking, worked on a plain-weave background. It uses a thin supplementary warp thread to fix the supplementary pattern weft onto the background material (Figure 3-30). The pattern thread actually lies on top of the background, rather than being inserted into it as in half tapestry or conventional inlay, and it is not visible from the reverse side. Beautiful color blending is possible with this technique, which is much faster to work than traditional tapestry and combines well with many types of embroidery.

Woven inlay techniques such as this one, in which the pattern thread lies on top of the background fabric, are directly related to the couching techniques developed in the twelfth century to fix metal threads onto the surface of fabrics (see Figures 1-6 and 5-19). The hanging in Figure 3-31 has a design of widely spaced metallic threads "couched" to the background fabric by means of the Moorman technique, combined with stitchery.

Plain-Weave Tapestry

Tapestry, a weaver-controlled technique for producing multicolored designs in a weft-faced weave, can be enhanced in many ways by the addition of embroidery, either to lend a flat design element that would be difficult or time-consuming to weave or to bring texture to the relatively smooth weave.

In tapestry weaving, narrow warp-wise lines are difficult to fashion. For this reason, many tapestries are woven sideways so that vertical elements can be woven weft-wise. The bird on the tapestry in Figure C-8 is a relatively vertical design element, while the background has more horizontal elements. Rather than weaving the bird, the artist has embroidered it over the woven background, thus greatly facilitating the construction of the piece, as well as producing a slightly more three-dimensional effect.

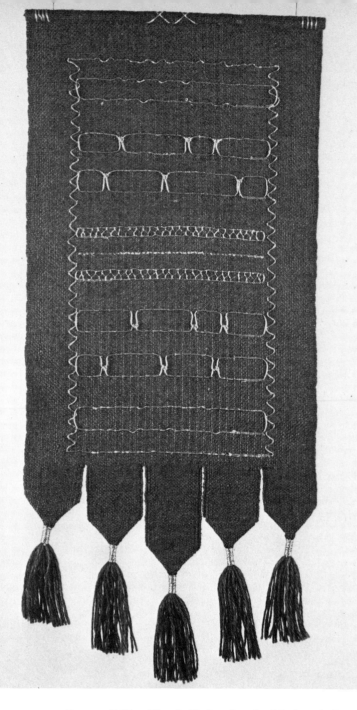

FIGURE 3-31. *"Couched" hanging by Marion Andrews. Metallic threads tied down to fabric surface by supplementary warp threads (Moorman technique). Interlaced bandstitch embroidered between rows of couched threads in center of piece.*

FIGURE 3-32. *Detached buttonhole filling, a needle-lace stitch. Shown worked over a single weft thread. Also can be worked out from a background fabric or over empty warp threads.*

Couching (described in the previous section) is an easy embroidery technique which can be used effectively with tapestry, both as a narrow outline and to cover a broader area. In *Splendor in the Hive* (Figure C-9), couching is used to outline areas of woven tapestry, echoing the pattern of loom-controlled honeycomb weave used elsewhere in the piece. A similar effect would have been difficult to achieve with weaving alone.

Lichen (Figures C-10 and C-11) illustrates how embroidery can be used to add texture and dimension to tapestry weaving. The tapestry itself was shaped on a frame loom, and then stuffed and quilted. Stitchery includes detached buttonhole filling (Figure 3-32), stemstitch (see Figure 1-3a) and featherstitch.

Detached buttonhole filling is a needle-lace stitch in which each row is looped into the previous one, forming a stretchy, textured surface. Needle-lace stitches can also be worked over a woven background (as in Figure 4-15), rather than out away from it, thus forming a second layer of fabric which can then be stuffed or used as pockets.

Needle lace, detached woven fillings (Figure 5-20) that also can be shaped and stuffed, Turkey work, raised needleweaving, and various textured embroidery stitches are employed in the traditional technique of stumpwork embroidery, where they are used to form three-dimensional designs and scenes. They all can be used in combination with tapestry or other weaves to achieve effects that would be difficult or impossible with weaving alone.

Basket Weave

Basket weave is another useful background for counted-thread embroidery. A draft for the two-harness version is given in Figure 3-33, although more complex setups on four or more harnesses are often used. Depending on yarn and sett, basket weave can produce a heavy or a lacy fabric. Because of the weave's coarseness, it is easier to count threads on it than on a plain weave of the same

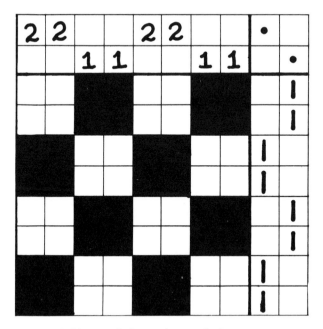

FIGURE 3-33. *Draft for two-harness basket weave.*

material and sett. The wool jacket shown in Figures C-21 and 5-11 has a basket-weave background, which was chosen because it is warmer and thicker than plain weave.

Basket weave and plain weave, of course, can easily be combined in the same woven piece, either by using the basic twill threading and appropriate treadling, or by threading the warp as desired for each section. All of the techniques for producing woven borders on plain weave can also be used with two-harness basket weave.

Twill

Twill fabrics can be used for embroidery in the same ways as plain-weave and basket-weave fabrics. They are most appropriate when a relatively heavy or stiff backing is desired, but because the warp and weft do not form a clearly defined perpendicular grid, twill is not as easy to use for counted-thread embroidery as plain and basket weave are. However, again, combining this weave with plain weave can result in interesting possibilities for embroidery (see Figure 4-3).

Canvas Weave

As one might suspect from its name, this weave is particularly suitable for canvas embroidery, though equally good for any other type of counted-threadwork. In *A Handweaver's Pattern Book* (see Bibliography), Marguerite P. Davison devotes an entire chapter to canvas weaves. One useful threading is given in Figure 3-34.

The rather widely spaced holes are conveniently well defined for ease in thread counting (Figure 3-35). However, unlike a plain weave set up to yield the same pattern of holes, canvas weave not only gives support for the embroidery but is also more supple than the traditional, commercially

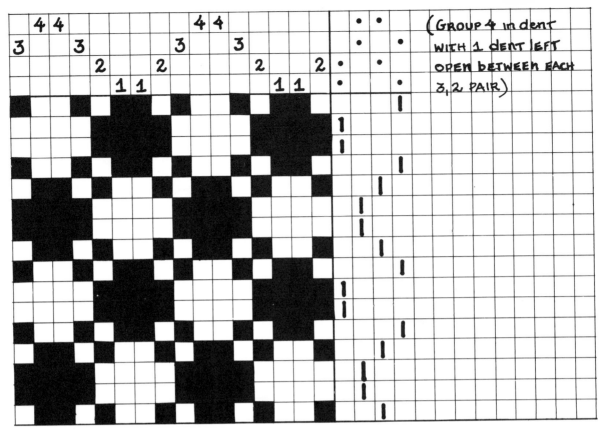

FIGURE 3-34. *Draft for a canvas weave.*

available needlepoint canvas. Traditional needlepoint canvas compensates for relatively wide spacing of threads by utilizing relatively stiff materials. Canvas weave is thus more suitable than needlepoint canvas for garments and other items where good draping quality is desired. Furthermore, commercial needlepoint canvas is not made to be seen, whereas a canvas-weave fabric need not be completely covered by needlepoint stitches in order to be attractive. Isolated designs can be applied to any portion of an item, leaving the background bare.

FIGURE 3-35. *Sample of crossstitch on a wool canvas weave. Evenly spaced holes formed by uneven sleying are convenient for counted-thread embroidery.*

Canvas weave, like plain weave, can be combined with other weaves and with various woven borders. It is appropriate for many types of clothing and is suitable for weaving in any fiber. In cotton or linen it was traditionally embellished with cross-stitch embroidery and used for towelling and table linens; in wool, it makes an excellent blanket fabric.

Huckaback and Other Float Weaves

Huckaback, one of the loom-controlled lace weaves, is traditionally characterized by staggered sets of floats. Many threadings and treadlings are given in *Four Harness Huck* (see Bibliography), by Evelyn Neher. A simple setup, which can be treadled in a number of different ways, is given in Figure 3-36. The first treadling sequence will result in alternating blocks of double floats, vertically aligned (warp-wise), formed by the threads on harnesses 2 and 3. The reverse of the material will display horizontally aligned pairs of floats. The second treadling sequence will give weft-wise floats on the upper side of the cloth. The weave can also be set up to give single or triple floats.

Traditionally, huckaback has been used for fine linen or cotton towels, and commercially available cotton huck comes in 15-inch widths for this purpose. A special type of embroidery (appropriately enough called "huck") evolved along with this weave, in which border designs are formed by threading colored yarns through the floats. Huck embroidery is one of the techniques classified as mock weaving. Figure 3-37 shows a traditional huck embroidery design offset by colored stripes, which is one way to "fancy up" huck needlework with woven embellishments.

FIGURE 3-36. *Draft for a huckaback weave with double floats.*

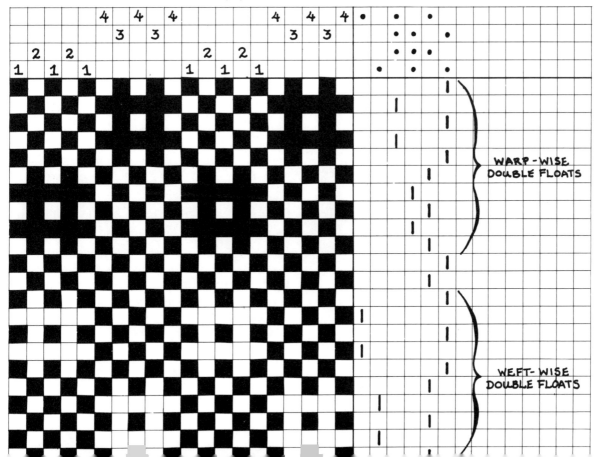

WARP-WISE DOUBLE FLOATS

WEFT-WISE DOUBLE FLOATS

FIGURE 3-37. *Sample of traditional huck embroidery on a huckaback fabric.*

FIGURE 3-38. *Tablecloth woven in plain weave and huckaback, embroidered with traditional huck embroidery pattern.*

As an embroiderer I had always looked down on huck embroidery, considering it a simpleminded, connect-the-dots exercise. As I explore the many treadling possibilities in the weave, however, I am coming to think of the embroidery technique as "simple" in the same sense that inlay weaving is: fast, easy, elegant, and versatile, with many possibilities for variations on a basic theme.

FIGURE 3-39. *Detail of tablecloth in Figure 3-38.*

By judicious threading and treadling, many effects can be achieved with handwoven huckaback that would not be available to embroiderers using commercially woven fabric. For instance, Figures 3-38 and C-12 show a small tablecloth woven in plain weave with a huckaback border in a different color. Along all four sides, the huckaback floats are perpendicular to the edge, allowing the embroidered design to face the edge (Figure 3-39). In this case, an eight-harness loom was used, with threading and treadling as in Figure 3-40a. (Clever weavers will be able to devise ways of achieving similar results with a four-harness loom.) Cotton thread (20/2, sett at 30 epi) was used for the fabric, with 5/2 perle cotton for the embroidery. The threading and pattern stripes were designed so that the floats under which the embroidery yarn is inserted are white, the same color as the embroidery thread, although the background for the stitchery is blue. Thus, floats and embroidery yarn blend together in the design. If they were different colors, the floats would show up more distinctly.

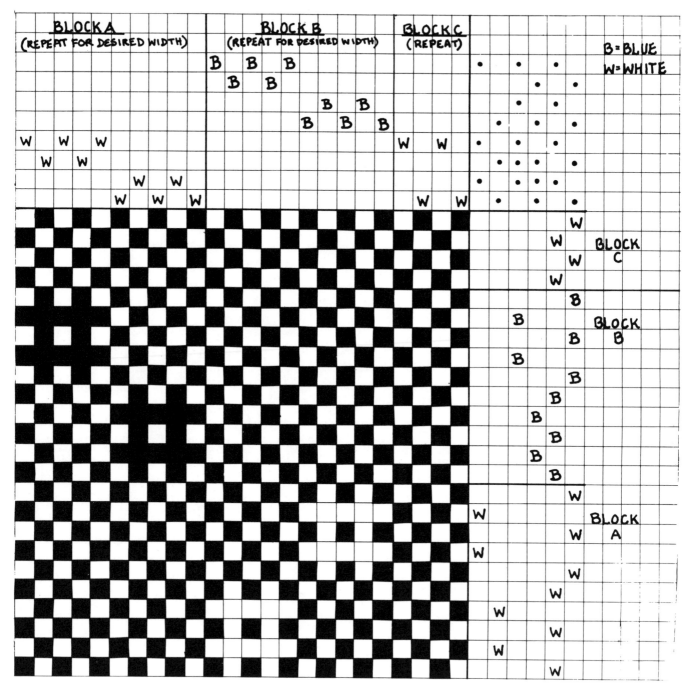

FIGURE 3-40a. *Draft for tablecloth in Figure 3-38*.

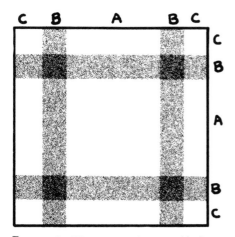

C B A B C
C
B
A
B
C

FIGURE *3-40b. Layout of pattern blocks.*

Most traditional huck embroidery motifs, even simple ones, require a dozen or more rows of background floats, and the embroidery threads may skip across several rows. Thus, for items intended for practical use rather fine materials and close sett (40 epi or more) are usually suitable for the background material as this will keep both design motifs and length of floats small. In contrast, huck embroidery with thick threads on a large-scale background could result in an object of significant visual impact. Here is another opportunity for the handweaver to experiment with a fabric design that is not commercially available.

Still another way to create a unique end product employing traditional embroidery designs would be to use wool threads in both fabric and embroidery, a technique appropriate for the border of a long skirt or for an afghan.

One type of traditional embroidery on huckaback looks very much like woven inlay. The pattern thread is merely inserted horizontally under the huck floats and carried back and forth to form designs, as shown in Figure 3-41. The second design from the left, worked on double floats, illustrates the texture typical of such embroidery on commercial huck fabric. Single- and triple-float huckaback (as illustrated by the first and third panels from the left) is ordinarily available only to the handweaver.

FIGURE *3-41. Sampler of huckaback woven and embroidered in a nontraditional manner.* From left: *single floats, double floats, triple floats, single floats woven with thin thread to hold down embroidered pattern threads unobtrusively (color blending used, in imitation of Moorman technique), and alternating vertical and horizontal double floats with warp-wise and weft-wise embroidered threads.*

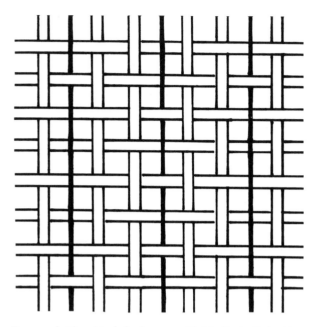

FIGURE 3-42. *Huckaback weave with thin floats. Embroidery yarns may be threaded through them for an effect similar to that of Moorman technique. Compare with Figure 3-30.*

The fourth design from the left illustrates how one may utilize a single-float huck (or, alternatively, a long supplementary warp float) as the basis for an embroidered "pseudo-Moorman technique": thin vertical floats, woven in black, through which pattern yarns may be threaded (Figure 3-42).

Nontraditional treadling of a huckaback threading can be used as the basis for more creative needlework designs. Many effects are possible which are very similar to woven inlay or overlay designs, but which are more versatile because they can include both weft-wise and warp-wise pattern threads. The fifth design from the left in Figure 3-41 shows how patterns may be devised to take advantage of the structure of a huck fabric with alternating horizontal and vertical floats.

Embroidered mock-weaving designs such as this last one were popular around the turn of the century, but they were worked through the long floats of a waffle weave rather than on a huckaback with bidirectional floats. Neither weave is commonly available in this country at the present time. Other float weaves can also be used as backgrounds for embroidered designs. For instance, the small hanging in Figure 3-43 was woven in a warp-faced float weave, with white pattern threads embroidered into the floats after completion of the weaving.

FIGURE 3-43. *Detail of hanging by Martha Davenport. Warp-faced float weave with embroidered pattern threads.*

FIGURE 3-44. *Rug. Double corduroy weave, with embroidered Ghiordes knots forming constellation patterns.*

The weaver may find that using a float weave and embroidery is preferable to using woven inlay, in several different ways. In addition to easy insertion of both weft-wise and warp-wise design elements, the combined technique may save time. Embroidered "overlay" designs on float weaves ordinarily go much faster than woven inlaid or overlaid patterns. Even if the background is handwoven, the weaver loses no time during weaving by stopping every few picks to lay a pattern thread, and the embroidering itself proceeds quickly, since the pattern thread is easily inserted under the floats, making it unnecessary to count threads. On the other hand, inlay into a tabby or other small-scale pattern shed will proceed more quickly if woven than if embroidered, particularly if long weft-wise pattern threads are being inserted.

Woven Pile (Corduroy)

The loom-controlled corduroy technique, in which long weft floats are cut to form the pile surface, is a tremendous time-saver in weaving pile rugs. Nonetheless, design possibilities are more limited than in knotted rugs, where a new color may be inserted with every knot. By combining weaving and embroidery, however, one can obtain much greater design freedom without great sacrifice of speed.

FIGURE 3-45. *Double-woven sample with alternating light and dark surfaces. Pattern woven in Brooks bouquet technique.*

FIGURE 3-46. *Double-woven sample with alternating light and dark surfaces. Embroidered patterns over light areas utilize satinstitch, eyelets, knotting, and needleweaving.*

For instance, the small rug in Figure 3-44 and C-13 could be produced either by embroidering Ghiordes (Turkey) knots on a previously woven backing or by producing the knots as the backing was woven. Actually, the dark blue pile background was woven in Peter Collingwood's double corduroy technique. After completion of the weaving, knots were embroidered to form the constellation patterns.

Double Weave

In double cloth, two separate surfaces are woven simultaneously. They may be manipulated to exchange position, the lower surface being brought above the former upper one, either across the entire width of the fabric or in selected areas to form designs. Weavers often combine techniques such as leno, Spanish lace (see Figure 4-7) or Brooks bouquet with double weave, using the lower woven surface as a background for the lacier upper surface (Figure 3-45). Similarly, embroidered lacy effects, such as achieved with pulled-thread and drawn-thread embroidery, can be used on the top surface of a double-woven material (Figure 3-46). An additional weaving technique that may be combined with stitchery is double-weave pickup, in which two surfaces in contrasting colors are interchanged to produce shaped pattern areas (Figure 3-47 a and b). Figures 3-46 and 3-48 a and b both include examples of double-weave pickup designs combined with embroidery.

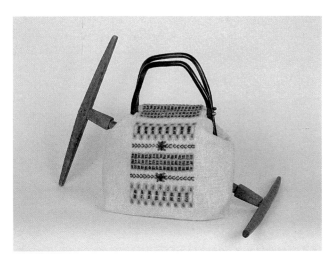

C-1. Sunflowers *by Ruth Dunlop Currey. Embroidery over plain weave.*

C-2. *Handbag by Maxine Boyd. Woven supplementary floats over plain weave, combined with embroidery.*

C-3. *Embroidery-weave (brocade) patterns overlaid on plain weave. Designed by Else Regensteiner from Greek peasant textiles in the Folk Art Museum at Thessaloniki, and woven by girls of the American Farm School in Thessaloniki. Photograph by Else Regensteiner.*

C-4. Bicentennial Caftan *by Nancy Arthur Hoskins. Woven overshot pattern. The scalloping detail at top of skirt border is done with needle and thread. Photograph by Blaine Hoskins.*

C-5. Freeze-up, Kabok River, Alaska *by Hazel Weed, design based on photograph by Manya Wik. Inlay and embroidery on plain weave.*

C-6. Trilliums *by Görel Kinersly. Half-tapestry weave with embroidery. Photograph by Lew Turner.*

C7. Tree by Penelope Drooker. Half-tapestry with twill pattern weft and embroidered French knots.

C-8. Loon by Carol Thilenius. Tapestry, background with bird embroidered in satin stitch. Photograph by artist.

C-9. Splendor in the Hive *by Barbara Jurgensen. Honeycomb weave, rya and flossa knotting, and tapestry with couched embroidery. Photograph by Barbara Minor. (Collection of Department of Fine Arts, Illinois State University, Normal.)*

C-10. Lichen *by Nancy Arthur Hoskins. Shaped tapestry with embroidery. including needle lace. Handspun green wool was dyed with lichen. Photograph by artist.*

C-11. Detail of C-10. Detached buttonhole filling, projecting out from tapestry. Photograph by artist.

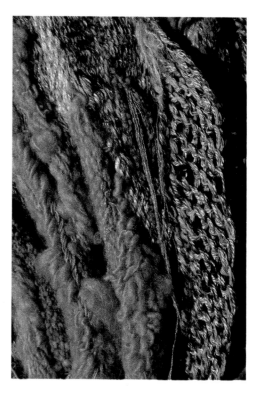

C-12. *Tablecloth in plain weave and huckaback by Penelope Drooker. Embroidery is traditional huck design.*

C-13. Winter Solstice, North by Northeast *by Penelope Drooker. Double corduroy weave with embroidered Ghiordes knots forming constellation patterns.*

C-14. Reversible double woven tunic by Penelope Drooker. Red side. Each diamond was embroidered with a different pulled-threadwork pattern. Photograph by artist.

C-15. Reversible double woven tunic. White side with Bargello embroidery. Photograph by artist.

C-16. Detail of tunic. Pulled-thread embroidery on double-weave pickup design. Photograph by artist.

C-17. Detail of tunic. Bargello embroidery on background of double-weave pickup design. Photograph by Bela Fixley.

C-18. Linen tunic by Penelope Drooker. Plain weave with open spaces left in warp and weft that were embroidered on the loom with drawn-threadwork designs.

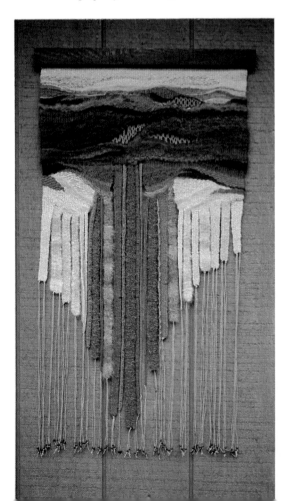

C-19. Placemat by Penelope Drooker. Plain weave with Brooks-bouquet design woven across fabric. The Brooks bouquet structure is duplicated by embroidery in warp-wise direction, and corner designs are embroidered in four-sided stitch.

C-20. Cascade by Nancy Arthur Hoskins. Tapestry with embroidery over unwoven warp threads, including needleweaving, Cretan open filling, and buttonhole stitch. Photograph by artist.

C-21. *Wool jacket by Penelope Drooker. Basket weave with embroidered threads over woven supplementary floats. Photograph by Michael S. Drooker.*

C-22. *Wool jacket, partially constructed with embroidery in progress. Photograph by Michael S. Drooker.*

C-23. *Monk's belt vest by Penelope Drooker. Woven float pattern with embroidered cross stitches.*

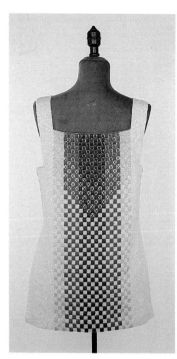

C-24. *Baby blanket by Penelope Drooker. Plain weave with warp-wise and weft-wise woven supplementary floats and embroidered diagonal lines. Photograph by Michael S. Drooker.*

FIGURES 3-47 a and b. Double-weave pickup design. The front (a) is exactly the opposite of the reverse (b).

FIGURES *3-48 a and b. Double-woven sample with picked-up pattern and embroidered designs. Dark threads were embroidered in Florentine stitch. Other embroidery stitches used were reverse wavestitch and buttonhole stitch. Reverse side (b) has no embroidery showing.*

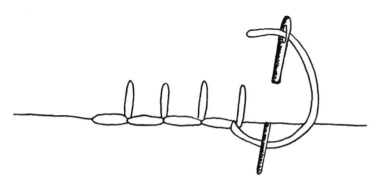

FIGURE *3-49. Buttonhole stitch.*

On a double-woven fabric consisting of two plain-weave surfaces, any type of embroidery requiring a plain-weave background can be utilized. Variation in fabric thread weight and sleying will produce a wide range of effects. Reversible items may be designed, in which two different embroidery techniques or patterns are used on the two surfaces of the double-woven fabric.

With a four-harness loom, two harnesses are allotted to each surface of a double weave. A versatile setup, which can be used for interchanging surfaces at will, is given in Figure 3-50. Alternating the two sequences of treadling will result in alternating stripes of black and white across the fabric, exactly opposite on each side.

To produce a more elaborate design with the interchanged surfaces, selected threads may be picked up from the bottom layer and brought to the surface; this process is often referred to as double-weave pickup. If desired, a design may be worked out on graph paper, with each square representing two warp threads and two weft threads of a given color or surface.

The only equipment needed to do double-weave pickup, aside from loom and shuttle, are two pickup sticks. Although sticks with bevelled edges are easiest to use, rulers or slats are satisfactory substitutes. For a black design on a white background, proceed as follows.

1. Treadle 1-3, raising black threads to surface. With stick, pick up all threads to be included in the first row of the design. Make a shed with the stick, and insert second stick under the same threads, behind the beater. Remove first stick, and release treadles.
2. Treadle 2, weaving with white.
3. Treadle 4, weaving with white. Remove pickup stick.
4. Treadle 2-4, raising white threads to surface. With stick, pick up all background threads for the first row of your design. Transfer threads to stick behind beater; release treadles.
5. Treadle 1, weaving with black.
6. Treadle 3, weaving with black. Remove pickup stick.

Continue as above, picking up design or background threads for subsequent rows of your design. (Although work goes faster if two picks of a given color are woven together, this is not necessary. If one pick is woven at a time, the pickup stick does not need to be transferred behind the beater, as it can simply be removed before beating.) Particularly if a reversible design is desired, care must be taken not to skip threads on the reverse side. A mirror comes in handy here.

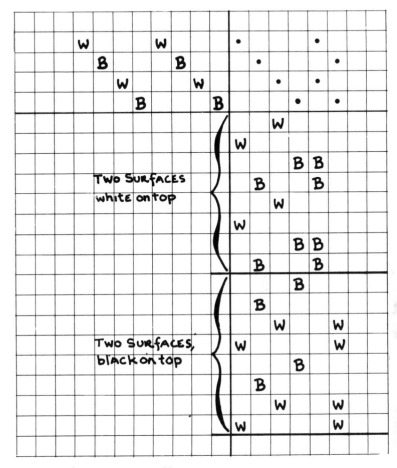

FIGURE 3-50. *Draft for double weave.*

With either stripes of interchanged fabric or more elaborate designs, embroidery on the upper surface can result in striking effects. Particularly suitable are drawn-thread and pulled-thread embroidery, which allow the lower surface to show through, but other techniques can be used also. Because the material is opaque, no embroidery need show on the reverse side. (Use a blunt needle to prevent catching unwanted threads.)

Comparison of the sample in Figure 3-46 with that in 3-48 will show the different effects achieved by using two different weights of thread for the two double-weave surfaces. The sample in Figure 3-48 uses threads of approximately the same weight (10/1 and 20/2 linen) for each surface; the sample in Figure 3-46, woven of 10/1 and 10/2 linen, gives a lacier effect.

Variations in spacing of warp or weft threads or both on one surface or another can be used very effectively in combination with embroidery. At the top of the sampler in Figure 3-51 are two examples of non-uniform sleying. Note that the first one, a widely spaced plain weave, does not hold its structure well. In the embroidered section (at the left), however, the structure holds its shape. Although the embroidery thread itself is difficult to see, its influence is apparent. Below this is a portion of the upper surface woven as mesh, by the draft in Figure 3-52. The mesh has been partially embroidered with a drawn-threadwork design, which changes the section's appearance considerably.

Figure 3-53 shows a sampler of designs embroidered over blocks of four-thread mesh on the upper surface of a double weave. Many different textures can be achieved. These blocks are not picked-up designs—though they could have been—but were woven on a multiharness loom. Although not nearly as versatile as picked-up patterns, loom-controlled double-woven block patterns can be created much more quickly.

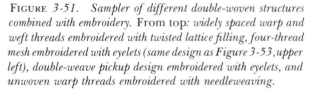

FIGURE 3-51. *Sampler of different double-woven structures combined with embroidery. From top: widely spaced warp and weft threads embroidered with twisted lattice filling, four-thread mesh embroidered with eyelets (same design as Figure 3-53, upper left), double-weave pickup design embroidered with eyelets, and unwoven warp threads embroidered with needleweaving.*

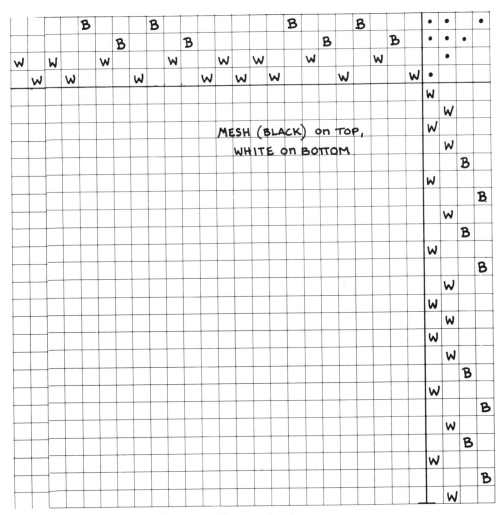

MESH (BLACK) on TOP,
WHITE on BOTTOM

FIGURE 3-52. *Draft for double weave with one surface in a four-thread mesh.*

FIGURE 3-53. *Sampler of drawn-thread embroidery designs on double-woven fabric with one surface in four-thread mesh.*

FIGURES 3-54 a, b, and c. Double woven reversible tunic. Picked-up design around yoke was embroidered differently on each side: (a) red slide, front; (b) red side, back; and (c) white side.

There is no need to be confined by a regular mesh. Any combination of warp and weft spacing could be used on the surface to be embroidered. Indeed, one could experiment with uneven spacing on both surfaces.

Figures 3-54, 3-55 and 3-56 and C-14 through C-17 show the design and construction of a reversible double-woven cotton tunic. The yoke was designed with a picked-up pattern of diamonds and stripes embellished with pulled-threadwork on the red side (white design) and with Florentine embroidery on the white side. The pulled-threadwork was completed on the loom, each diamond being decorated with a different stitch or pattern. That particular geometric shape was chosen to take advantage of the many pulled-threadwork stitches that develop along the diagonal. Embroidery on the white side was done off the loom but before the garment was sewn together.

As can be seen in the layout (Figure 3-56). the

tunic was designed, within the limitations of a 36-inch loom width, to require as few seams as possible. Actual weaving was from back to front. Two short cuts were made at the bottom back of the sleeves, then the side panels were brought around to meet the front panel. The garment was sewn under the arms and along the front panel, with satin stitch used for joining (red on red side, white on white side) and worked to completely cover the cut edges along the bottom of the sleeve.

Double-woven fabrics are, naturally, much heavier than a corresponding single layer of cloth. Thus, items appropriate for this technique include such things as placemats, bedspreads, handbags, pillows, and wall hangings. The reversible designs of double weaves lend themselves to items such as room dividers. If very open effects are achieved on the upper layer, such as in Figure 3-53, a double-woven fabric might be considered for a lampshade or window screen.

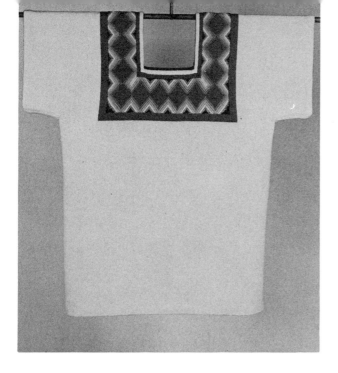

FIGURE 3-55. *Detail of reversible tunic. Pulled-thread embroidery on picked-up woven design (back of red side).*

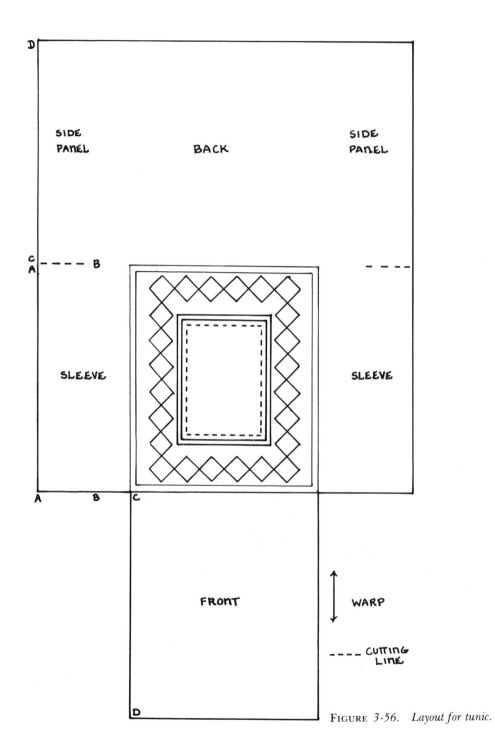

FIGURE 3-56. *Layout for tunic.*

48

CHAPTER 4

Embroidery over Unwoven Warp or Weft Threads

A NUMBER of traditional techniques usually classified as weaving involve either the manipulation of unwoven warp threads or the use of a weft thread that wraps around warp threads in various patterns rather than merely interlacing with them. Examples of the former would be gauze or leno (see Figure 1-4) and Brooks bouquet (see Figure 3-45), while soumak and twining (see Figure 4-24) exemplify the latter.

All of these woven structures have their counterparts in embroidery. Gauze patterns used by weavers in combination with plain weave to form leno are also used by embroiderers in drawn-threadwork, as are the sheaflike structures typical of the Brooks-bouquet weave. Stemstitch in embroidery has exactly the same structure as soumak weaving, the only difference being that stemstitch is worked over an interlaced background fabric, while soumak is worked over empty warp threads. Many additional structures traditionally thought of as embroidery stitches may also be worked over empty warp or weft threads, forming unique textural effects completely integrated with the fabric structure. For instance, many needle lace stitches are easily adapted to this technique.

This chapter describes some of the unique textures achieved by working embroidery stitches directly over empty warp or weft threads, rather than on a woven background. Manipulating or distorting exposed warp or weft threads results in a lacy, open texture, while wrapping or enclosing empty warp or weft threads with embroidered structures without altering their position may produce either an opaque, textured surface or a lacy pattern, depending on the size and spacing of the embroidery yarn. A summary outline relating embroidery stitches to woven structures and detailing the opaque or lacy appearance of each can be found at the end of the book.

Manipulated Warp or Weft Threads

In leno weaving (Figure 4-1a), sections of plain weave alternate with sections (called gauze) of warp threads which have been transposed and held in place with widely spaced weft threads.

A similar open effect is achieved in drawn-thread embroidery. With that technique, however, the embroiderer starts with a piece of plain-weave fabric and then cuts and draws out warp or weft threads (hence, the name) to leave sections of bare, unwoven threads. Finally, these bare threads are manipulated to form lacy patterns.

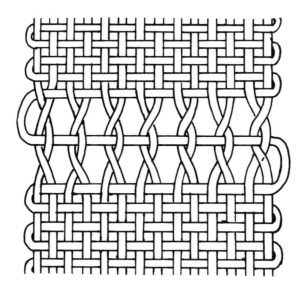
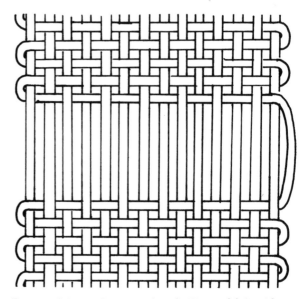

FIGURE 4-1. *a. Leno weaving; b. Woven fabric with empty warp threads, designed for subsequent embroidery.*

The relationship between drawn-thread embroidery and woven leno is one which can be traced back to sixteenth-century Scandinavia, where the scarcity of looms led to the practice of completing the manipulation of empty warp threads off the loom, thus saving weaving time; this gradually evolved into a wide variety of embroidery techniques including Hardanger work and näversöm work, among others.

Weavers may well find it advantageous to reverse this process by doing embroidery on the loom in the same way they do leno. Thus, instead of tediously cutting and withdrawing threads from a woven fabric as embroiderers must do to prepare it for traditional drawn-thread embroidery or needleweaving, it is possible to create a background material having spaces in the desired positions (Figure 4-1b). Although this process is similar to leno, the difference is that empty warp threads are manipulated and secured, not with the weft thread as the piece is being woven, but after the surrounding background has been completed and with a separate thread.

With embroidery, more intricate designs are possible than can be achieved with the traditional leno technique. In addition, not only warp threads (as in leno) but also weft threads can be manipulated and secured by the embroidery thread (see Figure 1-5).

FIGURE 4-2. *Hemstitch.*

In much drawn-thread embroidery, the edges of the open spaces are secured by hemstitching (Figure 4-2) or other stitches such as satinstitch or reverse wavestitch before the warp or weft threads are manipulated. The purpose is not only to keep the weft or warp threads from slipping into the open space but also to group the threads for additional decorative effect. Although this process is more time-consuming than the weaving of leno, a greater variety of effects can be achieved.

Figure 4-3 shows a sampler of embroidery worked on a plain-weave background with portions of warp threads left unwoven. Several of the embroidered strips have specially woven borders to set them off. Of special note is the fact that designs in both openwork weaving and openwork embroidery are formed as much by the negative space (holes) surrounding the manipulating threads as they are by the threads themselves.

If precisely measured unwoven spaces are desired, a knitting needle or slat can be inserted across the material as the weaving progresses; if not (or for small spaces), light use of the beater should suffice. For embroidery done on the loom, a slight slackening of tension is advisable to allow for takeup of the manipulated threads. Just as for leno, tension problems may arise in the warp if there are large embroidered sections which do not extend across the entire width of the fabric.

FIGURE 4-3. *Sampler of drawn-thread embroidery designs worked over unwoven warp threads. From top: herringbone and four-sided stitches in conjunction with a border woven over alternate pairs of warp threads; needleweaving in shaped opening in weft threads; wrapped cording bordered by twill weave; four-sided stitch bordered by pick-and-pick design; needleweaving; knotted design; and woven webs over knotted and hemstitched groups bordered by colored stripes.*

FIGURE 4-4. *Tunic. Plain weave with open spaces left in warp and weft was embroidered on the loom with drawn-threadwork designs.*

FIGURE 4-5. *Detail of tunic in Figure 4-4. Four-sided stitch and woven webs, with reverse wavestitch used to group threads for webs.*

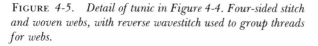

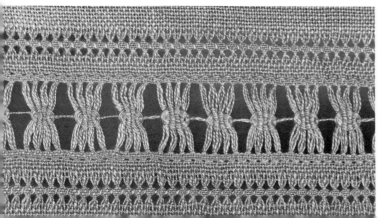

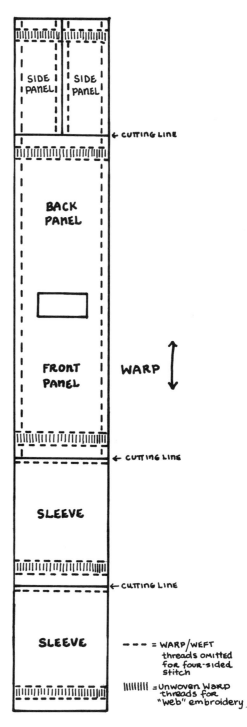

FIGURE 4-6. *Layout of tunic.*

The linen tunic shown in Figures 4-4 and C-18 was woven in tabby, leaving weft-wise and warp-wise open spaces for pulled-thread and drawn-thread designs along bottom, sleeves, and seams. It was embroidered entirely on the loom, using the same linen thread as for warp and weft. Embroidery patterns employed were four-sided stitch, woven webs, and reverse wavestitch, which was used to hold the groups of threads for the webs. A detail of the embroidery is shown in Figure 4-5. Layout of the garment is diagrammed in Figure 4-6.

Naturally, woven openwork designs can be combined with embroidered ones. For instance, to form a four-sided border, a design of weft-wise woven leno, warp bouquet, or Spanish lace (Figure 4-7) could be duplicated by embroidery in the warp-wise direction (Figures 4-8, 4-9, and C-19). Because warp threads are attached to the loom, it is impossible to manipulate weft threads by using warp threads, and embroidery must be used instead.

For some traditional embroidery techniques, a background is produced by withdrawing threads in two directions from a tabby fabric, rather than in a single direction, forming a mesh (Figure 4-10). Of course, such a mesh, with grouped warp and weft, can be produced directly on the loom. Examples of traditional needlework techniques worked over such a loom-created background are illustrated in Figure 4-11. The mesh was sleyed 2,2,0,0. Patterns such as those in Figure 3-53 also can be worked on a plain-weave mesh.

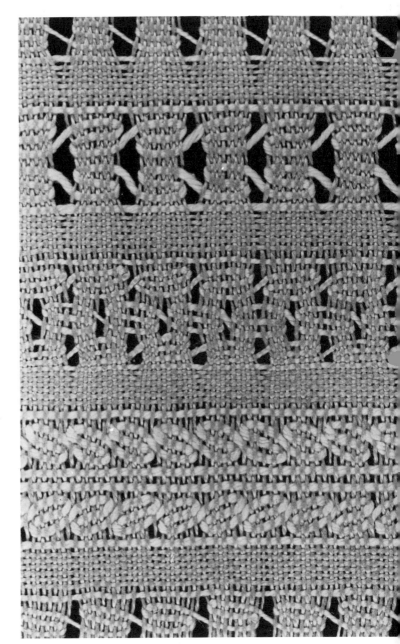

FIGURE 4-7. *Portion of Spanish-lace sampler. These weft-wise woven patterns can be duplicated by embroidery in the warp-wise direction.*

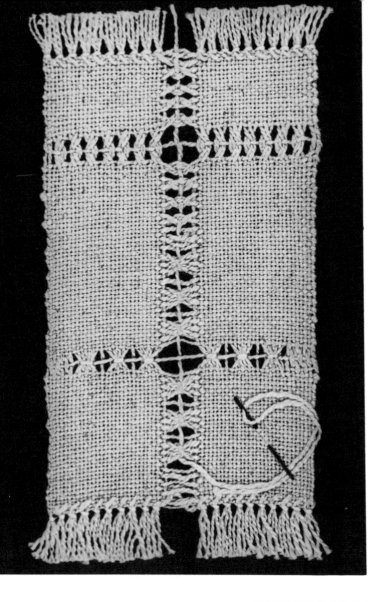

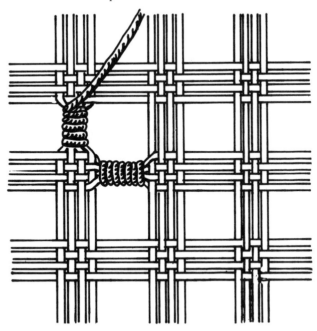

FIGURE 4-8. Sample of woven openwork (weft-wise) combined with and duplicated by embroidery (warp-wise). Top: leno; bottom: Brooks bouquet.

FIGURE 4-10. Mesh fabric. Produced either by cutting and withdrawing threads from balanced plain weave, or by spacing warp and weft during weaving. Wrapping (cording)—as used in Hardanger and Sicilian embroidery—is shown in progress.

FIGURE 4-9. Placemat. Brooks-bouquet design woven across fabric is duplicated by embroidery in warp-wise direction. Corner designs are embroidered in four-sided stitch.

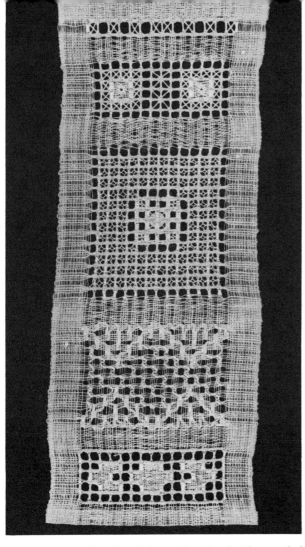

Although traditional drawn-threadwork patterns predominate in the various samplers in this chapter, these designs can be used in ways far removed from traditional embroidery. For instance, in combination with tapestry weaving, drawn-threadwork designs contrast strongly with the opaque, weft-faced areas. Such an effect can be seen in *Cascade* (Figure C-20), where needleweaving in the upper blue areas has been used to give the impression of foaming, flowing water.

Enclosed Warp or Weft Threads

Weavers obtain texture in their work by a variety of different methods, including various pattern weaves, combinations of different-sized yarns, pile weaves (cut or looped), and soumak (see Figure 1-3b). Figure 4-12 shows a soumak sampler with many different texture effects.

FIGURE 4-11. *Sampler of drawn-thread embroidery worked over a woven mesh.* From top: *Two corded (wrapped) patterns typical of Hardanger embroidery (second design is supplemented by woven squares of material in the same thread as the background; in traditional Hardanger work, such opaque areas are left in the cloth as threads are withdrawn around them); design in cording, needleweaving, woven web, and loop stitch; design typical of Scandinavian näversöm embroidery in diagonal stitch and ground stitch; and Sicilian drawn-thread embroidery with rewoven design areas.*

FIGURE 4-12. *Soumak sampler.* From top: *alternating colors, tapestry in Egyptian knot and soumak, vertical soumak (single and double), and variety of textures created by "stitch" spacing and slant.*

FIGURE 4-13. *Greek Vase by Bucky King. Wool tapestry, including Egyptian knot, Ghiordes knot, wrapped soumak, and several variations of chain stitch. Photograph by W. S. King.*

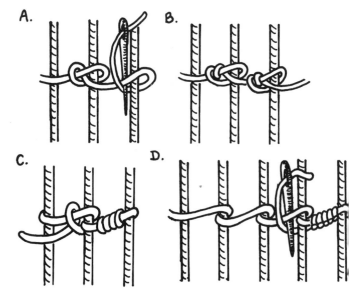

FIGURE 4-14. *Variations of soumak, worked with needle: (a) One loop, (b) two loops, (c) wrapped, and (d) buttonhole stitch over soumak.*

Embroidery also may be employed to achieve texture. Many of the stitches for manipulating warp or weft threads, discussed in the previous section, as well as others, may be worked over warp threads to hide them completely, resulting in an opaque, textured surface.

Though the idea may seem innovative to today's fiber worker, a similar combination of stitchery and weaving was employed as early as the eighth century on middle-eastern work. In this century, Bucky King has been a leader in combining embroidery with tapestry techniques, focusing on variations of chainstitch, buttonhole stitch, and soumak (Figure 4-13).

The sampler in Figure 4-15 illustrates a few of the traditional embroidered structures which may be worked directly over warp threads for textured effects. Here, narrow sections of embroidery have

FIGURE 4-15. *Sampler of embroidery stitches combined with weft-faced plain weave. From top:* detached buttonhole filling, spaced buttonhole filling, and knotted buttonhole filling; Ceylon stitch; uncut Ghiordes knots, some with buttonhole stitch; double lock (cable) stitch, pulled tightly; Cretan open filling; double lock (cable) stitch; checkered chain band; twisted chain stitch; raised chain band; chain stitch; and two rows of soumak.

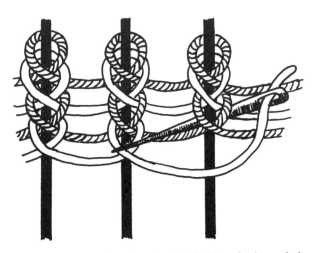

FIGURE 4-16. *Ceylon (loop, rib) stitch. May also be worked without support threads.*

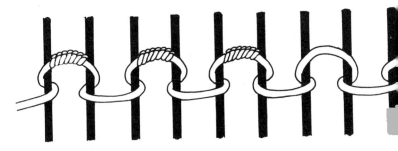

FIGURE 4-17. *Buttonhole stitch over uncut Ghiordes knots.*

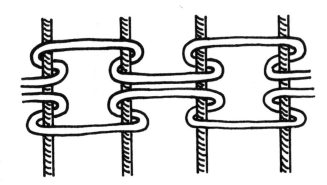

FIGURE 4-18. *Double lock (cable) stitch.*

been set off by wider bands of weft-faced plain weave. For an overall texture, however, many rows of stitchery may be worked in succession, each separated by only one or two rows of plain weave. Note that the soumak at the bottom appears identical to the row of chain stitch; only by looking at the reverse side can the two easily be distinguished. The checkered chain band (fifth from bottom) has the same structure as weft twining. (All of the stitches listed as band stitches will be met again in the next chapter, this time worked over supplementary floats against a background of balanced plain weave.) If you look closely, you can see that the uncut Ghiordes knot (third section from top) wraps around the warp threads in the same way as the threads that make up the cablestitch (fourth from top); the latter is pulled tightly, whereas the former is worked loosely, leaving a loop of thread on the surface.

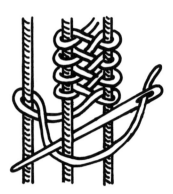

FIGURE 4-19. *Cretan open filling.*

FIGURE 4-21. *Twisted chain stitch. Same structure as coral stitch and as knots used in drawn-thread embroidery.*

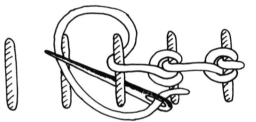

FIGURE 4-22. *Raised chain band.*

1.   **2.**

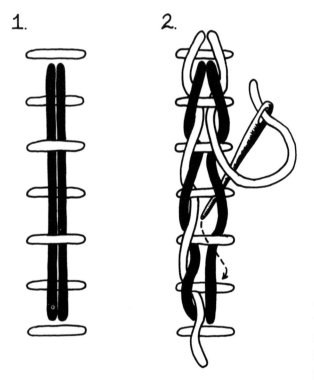

FIGURE 4-20. *Checkered chain band (as worked over fabric).*

The three buttonhole fillings at the top of the sampler are examples of needle-lace stitches. Here, they have been worked out from a woven background, and could be stuffed for a three-dimensional effect or used as pockets. Such looped stitches are very stretchy. They can be shaped, both three dimensionally (out from the fabric) and two dimensionally (where they are attached to the background fabric, their outlines can be any shape).

Needle-lace stitches can also be worked directly over empty warp threads, rather than out from a woven background. Most are easiest to work running parallel to the warp threads (Figure 4-24), but many (such as Ceylon stitch) can be worked perpendicular to the support threads. Both opaque, textured effects and delicate, lacy effects can be achieved, depending on choice of thread and stitch spacing.

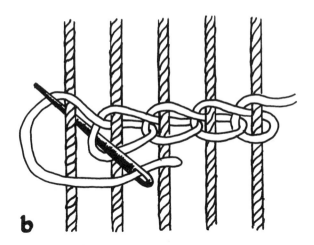

FIGURE 4-23. *Chain stitch: (a) over fabric; (b) over warp threads. This stitch has same structure as weft chaining, in which the weft is looped over warp threads without use of a needle.*

FIGURE 4-24. *Sample of needle lace stitches worked over horizontal support threads. Sides are secured by rows of twining. From top: buttonhole filling, diamond stitch, knotted buttonhole* filling (all worked in thin threads); chevron stemstitch (note influence of stitch spacing on effect created); and buttonhole filling and knotted buttonhole filling worked in heavy yarn.

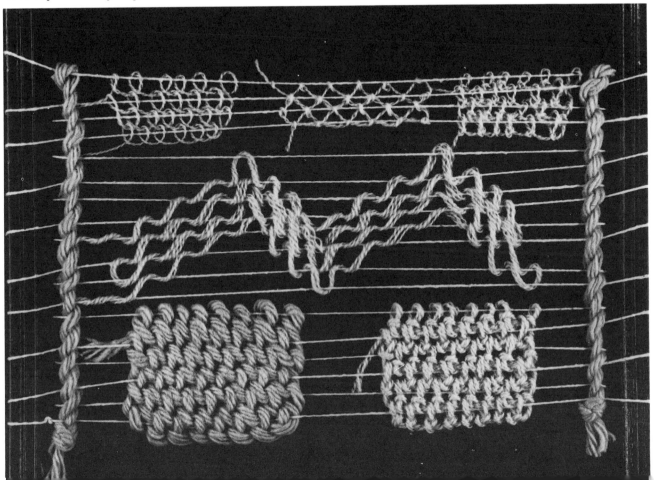

Detached filling stitches (a few of which are shown in Figure 5-20) are another group of structures which, like needle lace, can be worked either out from a woven background for a three-dimensional effect or directly over empty warp threads for a lacier effect.

Weaves other than weft-faced plain weave, such as balanced plain weave or twill, can, of course, be used in combination with embroidery stitches that enclose warp threads. The notebook cover in Figure 4-25 was woven in a lightweight twill and decorated with embroidery stitches worked over warp threads as the weaving progressed. Such stitches can also be worked over empty weft threads, in the same manner as illustrated in Figure 4-8, and weft-wise and warp-wise stripes can be combined to form frames, borders, or other bidirectional designs.

Summary of Embroidery Stitches and Techniques

Though space does not allow more detailed examination of the use of embroidery directly over unwoven warp or weft threads, I hope that the few examples given will spark the imaginations of both weavers and embroiderers. There are endless possibilities here for original, creative combinations of stitchery and weaving. The outline at the end of the book lists many such embroidery stitches and techniques. It summarizes both structural relationships and appearance of individual stitches (which may vary according to embroidery thread and/or stitch spacing used). Most of the stitches listed but not diagrammed in this chapter and the outline can be found in *Needle Lace and Needleweaving*, by Jill Norfors (see Bibliography).

FIGURE 4-25. *Notebook cover. Twill weave, with embroidery stitches (twisted chain stitch, raised chain band, cable stitch) worked over warp threads as weaving progressed.*

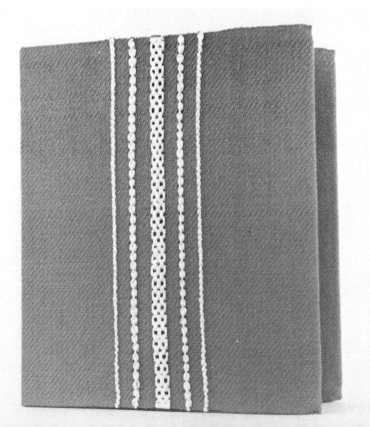

CHAPTER 5

Woven Floats as the Basis for Embroidery Stitches

IN CONTRAST to fabrics which serve solely as backgrounds for decorative embroidery, woven materials may be designed to include elements—floats—which serve as parts of the embroidery stitches themselves. Any embroidery stitch that includes a vertical or horizontal element, and there are many, can be produced partially or entirely on the loom. The great majority of them are included in the broad category of counted-thread embroidery.

Since the most tedious and time-consuming part of counted-thread embroidery is, as one might expect, the counting of threads to obtain evenly spaced, appropriately sized stitches, it is evident that using the loom to do the counting—in effect, setting up a mechanical system to define the stitches—can result in a tremendous saving of time.

After a portion of the stitch has been woven along with the background fabric, the design can be completed rapidly with needle and thread (see Figure 1-10). Producing embroidery stitches in this way goes so quickly that it may be considered even for use on handwoven production items.

Over a period of time, I have collected a group of embroidery stitches appropriate for use on woven floats. Certainly there are many more candidates for inclusion, and I am continually adding to my list.

Many of these stitches, along with the floats on which they are based, have been worked on a series of samplers illustrated in this chapter. Also included are drafts of weaves that can be used to produce the floats, as well as a general discussion of how to go about planning and designing items which make use of "woven" embroidery stitches. At the end of the book is an outline summarizing the relationships between such stitch structures and woven structures.

The most obvious woven structure for the production of counted-thread embroidery stitches is a plain weave with supplementary warp or weft threads or both added in a loom-controlled pattern or in a picked-up shed. Monk's belt, the simplest example of this type of pattern threading, can give an exact imitation of the structure of the running stitch in embroidery on plain weave. In turn, the running stitch is the basis for numerous embroidery stitches and techniques. Every one of the counted-thread stitches considered in the following pages can be produced by use of supplementary floats, with loom-controlled elements being embellished by needlework. Other woven structures, however, such as double weave or float weaves, may also be used to produce portions of embroidery stitches with the loom.

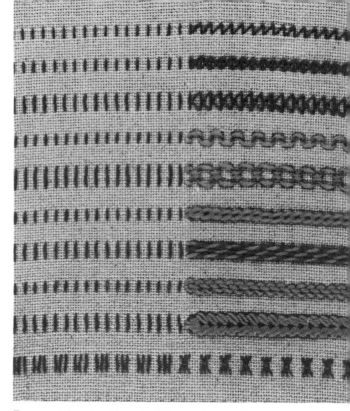

FIGURE 5-2. *Sampler of stitches embroidered over woven floats which are perpendicular to linear direction of stitch.* From top: *Bosnian stitch, cross stitch with bar, triangle stitch, lockstitch, double lockstitch (cablestitch), stemstitch band, woven bandstitch (one of several possible designs), raised chain bandstitch, Portuguese border stitch, and sheafstitch.*

FIGURE 5-1. *Sampler of stitches embroidered over woven floats which are parallel to linear direction of stitch.* From top: *single threaded (laced) running stitch, double threaded (laced) running stitch, single whipped running stitch, double whipped running stitch, guilloche stitch (includes double threaded running stitch and French knots), brick and cross (one row), double back-laced running stitch, interlaced running stitch (based on Cretan stitch), whipped double running (overcast) stitch, single-threaded (laced) double running stitch, double-threaded (laced) double running stitch, Pekinese stitch, double Pekinese stitch, and raised Cretan stitch.*

Most embroidery stitches are constructed to give either clearly defined linear designs, most often used to form border patterns, or to cover broad areas of fabric. The woven framework for stitches within these two categories may be set up quite differently. I have, therefore, divided my discussion into two major sections, Linear Designs and Overall Designs. In many cases, of course, linear stitches can be grouped to cover large areas, while overall designs can be adapted to form borders. I give you here only the stitches themselves, and leave it to you to design combinations and variations to suit the purposes of your own projects.

Embroidery Stitches for Linear Designs

Figures 5-1, 5-2, and 5-6 illustrate embroidery stitches particularly appropriate for use in border designs. On the left side of each photograph are the basic floats as they would be woven; on the right are the completed embroidery stitches.

In most of the stitches shown, the embroidery thread merely laces through or around the woven float, rather than piercing the background fabric. Even where the thread does pass back and forth through the fabric, its position is predetermined by the woven floats, so that the needlework proceeds rapidly.

Three general types of float structure are clearly illustrated in the three samplers: parallel to the linear direction of the stitch (shown as horizontal), perpendicular to the linear direction of the stitch (shown as vertical), or bidirectional—vertical and horizontal floats used together.

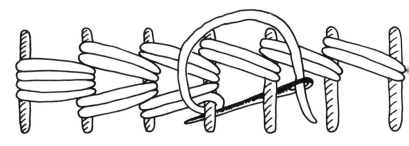

FIGURE 5-4. *Portuguese border stitch.*

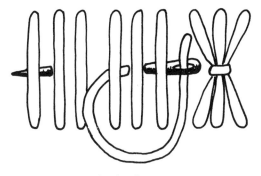

FIGURE 5-5. *Sheafstitch.*

FIGURE 5-3. *Woven bandstitch.*

FIGURE 5-6. *Sampler of embroidery stitches based on vertical and horizontal floats used together.* From top: *Holbein-work design, St. George and St. Andrew, diamond cross stitch, and reversed double cross stitch.*

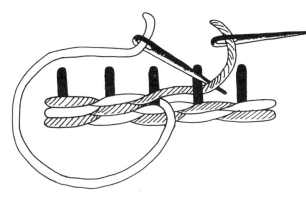

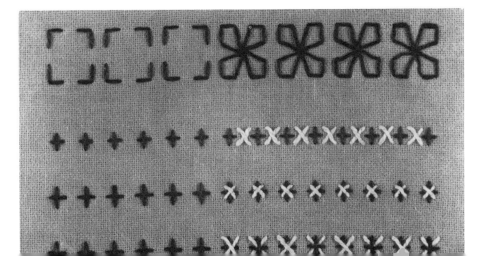

The first group of stitches (Figure 5-1) is based on the running stitch and double running stitch (two alternating rows of running stitch, which together make a solid line). Many of the stitches are very closely related; for instance, the double-threaded running stitch and the double-threaded double running stitch have exactly the same structure except for the float patterns on which they are based. (The design on the wool jacket in Figures 5-11 and C-21 is made up entirely of stitches based on single running stitch.)

Figure 5-2 shows a large group of stitches based on vertical floats. Most of these stitches are detached from the background, and several show very close relationships to weaving, as noted in Chapter 4. Drawn-thread embroidery designs and needle-weaving can also be done over vertically oriented floats, rather than over empty warp threads as usually done.

Stitches in Figure 5-6 are based on bidirectional floats. At the top is an example of a Holbein-work design incorporating both horizontal and vertical floats, with additional diagonal floats embroidered in. A great number of interesting designs can be devised within this framework; in fact, interesting patterns can be devised even working with only vertical or horizontal lines plus diagonals (see Figure 1-10e).

The rest of the stitches in Figure 5-6 are based on the straight cross stitch. All of the basic crosses can be produced either entirely by the loom or by embroidering perpendicular lines over floats woven in a single direction.

Woven Structures for Linear Design

Two types of weaves are most useful in producing floats for linear-design embroidery stitches:

1. Woven supplementary floats in a color contrasting with the main weave, weft-wise or warp-wise, either over plain weave or over other backgrounds such as basket weave or twill;
2. Twill weave, with selected weft or warp threads woven in a color contrasting with that of the background.

With woven supplementary floats, the colored float is separate from the structure of the background fabric, merely an addition to it, but in the twill weave, the float is an integral part of the woven structure.

WEAVER-CONTROLLED PICKUP

The most straightforward method of producing weft floats over a plain-weave background is by weaver-controlled pickup of warp threads, as done for brocade weaving on simple looms (shown in Figures 1-2 and C-3). This allows floats to be produced over any number of threads and in any pattern. It has little advantage over embroidery, however, as it is equally time-consuming. Indeed, as the inlay process considerably slows down the weaving process for the background material, a net time loss is probable. For special effects and small, isolated motifs, however, this technique should not be discounted.

It can be used also for overlaying long floats such as those required for couching (see Figure 1-6). Since the major effort in producing couched designs is in the needlework rather than the overlaid floats, however, very little time is gained by weaving the floats rather than embroidering them, and the choice is primarily a matter of personal preference.

LOOM-CONTROLLED UNIDIRECTIONAL
SUPPLEMENTARY FLOATS

The stitches shown in Figures 5-1, 5-2 and 5-6 are a completely different story. In every case, much

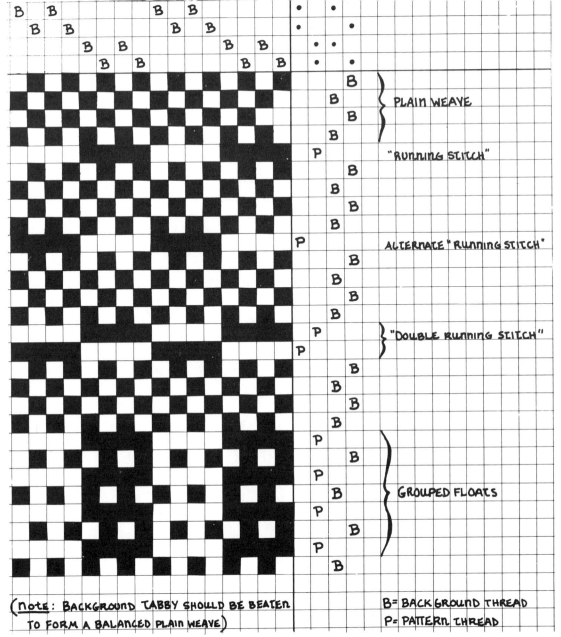

FIGURE 5-7. *A draft for weft-wise supplementary floats on plain weave. Threading determines float length.*

time may be gained by weaving the floats on which they are based, using a loom-controlled pattern to place them.

To exactly duplicate the structure of the running stitch on a plain-weave background, a monk's belt type threading may be used, for either weft-wise or warp-wise floats. Deciding between weft-wise and warp-wise floats depends on the design of the article to be woven, as well as on the weaver's own treadling preference.

The length of weft-wise floats is predetermined by the loom threading; position and color of pattern

FIGURE 5-8. *Variations in float length in a monk's belt threading.*

threads, however, may be determined at any time during the weaving. Two or more shuttles are used for this weave, one for the background weft and one or more for the pattern weft(s).

In contrast to weft-wise floats, the length of warp-wise floats may be varied at will, but the placement and color of pattern threads must be planned in advance and set up on the loom. As only a single shuttle is required, once the design is set up the weaving proceeds relatively rapidly.

A draft for weft-wise floats is given in Figure 5-7. Note that at least one tabby shot is always made between each pattern thread. Two harnesses are used for each group of threads to be raised for a given float pattern; thus, a four-harness loom can be set up to weave two alternating sequences of floats. This particular threading gives a four-thread skip for the pseudo-running stitch produced by the woven floats. Six, eight, or more threads can be set up as the float length, depending on the effect desired and the sett of the background fabric. Variations in pattern yarns and treadling sequence can give a great variety of patterns from this one simple threading.

FIGURE 5-9. *A draft for warp-wise supplementary floats on plain weave. Threading determines float position.*

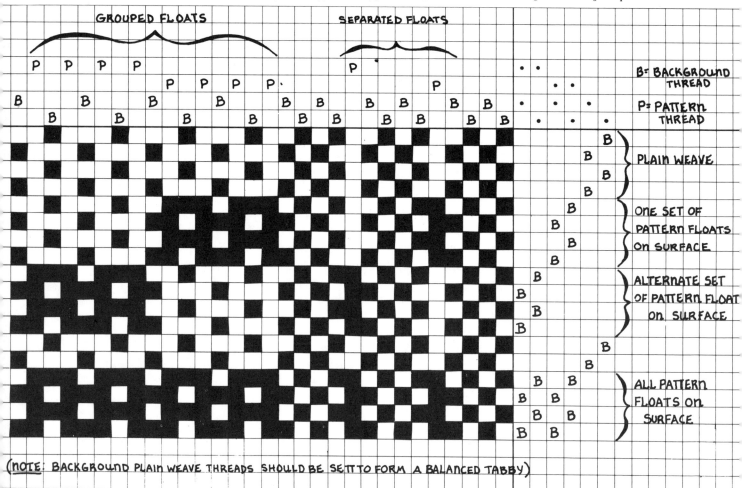

(NOTE: BACKGROUND PLAIN WEAVE THREADS SHOULD BE SET TO FORM A BALANCED TABBY)

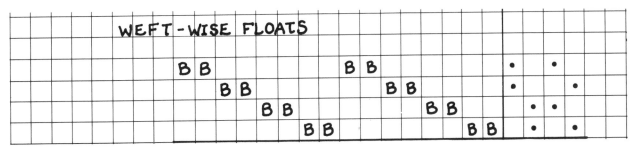

B= BACKGROUND THREAD
P= PATTERN THREAD

FIGURE 5-10. *Threadings for warp-wise and weft-wise supplementary floats on two-harness basket weave.*

Special effects or patterns can be achieved by varying the length of floats as set up on the loom (Figure 5-8). Pattern threads can cover the entire width of the fabric or be overlaid into selected smaller areas.

Corresponding to the threading for the production of weft-wise floats is a similar monk's belt setup for warp-wise floats. In this weave, two harnesses carry the tabby threads and one or more additional harnesses carry the pattern threads. For instance, in the draft shown in Figure 5-9, harnesses 3 and 4 carry the pattern threads. They may be raised at will—together or separately—to form the woven design. Figure 5-24 includes a small sample of warp-wise supplementary floats woven from this draft. The sample illustrates both grouped and spaced floats.

A separate tensioning device is almost a necessity if a long piece of fabric containing warp floats is to be woven, since pattern threads on the same beam as background threads will become relatively looser as weaving progresses because they do not interweave as often as the background threads. Usually tension on pattern threads should be kept relatively light but consistent. Particularly for embroidery stitches that are to be threaded or interlaced, the pseudo-running stitch produced by the woven floats should not be so tight that it puckers the background when the interlacing thread is inserted. This holds equally true for weft-wise pseudo-running stitches.

Supplementary floats, either warp-wise or weft-wise, may be overlaid on a background fabric other than plain weave. For instance, on a four-harness

FIGURE 5-11. *Wool jacket. Basket weave with embroidered threads over woven supplementary floats.*

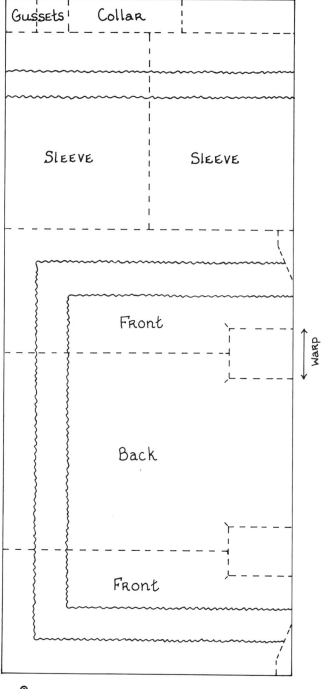

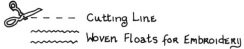

Cutting Line

Woven Floats for Embroidery

FIGURE 5-12. *Layout of wool jacket.*

loom a two-harness basket weave may be used. Threading for warp-wise or weft-wise floats could be set up as in Figure 5-10, with treadling similar to that for plain weave and spacing of floats varied according to the pattern chosen.

In an analogous way, a twill weave can be set up with supplementary floats. Except for the case of a three-harness twill with warp-wise supplementary floats controlled by a single pattern harness, more than four harnesses would be required for such a weave.

Several of the stitches pictured in Figure 5-1 (whipped running stitch, interlaced running stitch, and guilloche stitch) were combined into a border pattern and "woven" on a basket-weave background to decorate the wool jacket illustrated in Figures 5-11 and C-21. Since the design runs around the bottom and up the front of the garment, both warp-wise and weft-wise floats were required. Although a multiharness loom would have been handy for this project, one was not available, so heddle-stick harnesses (as used on frame and backstrap looms) were devised at the front of a four-harness loom to pick up warp threads for the weft-wise pattern floats. These were lifted by hand, but since they were used relatively infrequently this did not slow down the weaving significantly. Placement of weft-wise and warp-wise floats can be seen in the layout of the garment (Figure 5-12).

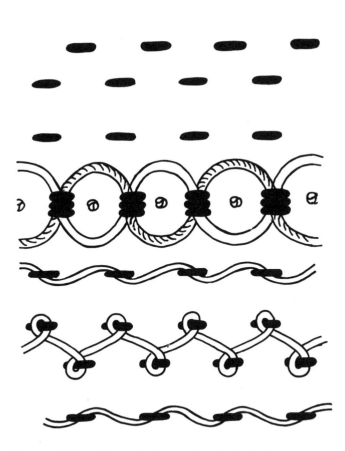

FIGURE 5-14. *Placement of woven floats for border design on wool jacket.*

FIGURE 5-13. *Detail of border design on wool jacket. Whipped running stitch, interlaced running stitch and guilloche stitch embroidered over woven floats.*

Figure 5-13 shows a detail of the border design, and Figure 5-14 shows its construction. (Never would I have embroidered such a design "from scratch"—the running stitches would have taken forever!) The partially completed jacket, with embroidery in progress, is shown in Figure C-22. The pattern of the woven floats is clearly visible. (Because they are not composed of vertical and horizontal elements, the diamond-shaped motifs on the sleeves were embroidered entirely by hand, using stitches similar to those in the border.)

As mentioned earlier, washing and pressing generally flatten out embroidery. For this reason, the jacket was washed, pressed, and sewn together (except for the lining) before the embroidery was done. Thus, seams and edges could be pressed without fear of flattening the stitchery.

Moorman technique, which uses supplementary warp threads to tie down supplementary weft threads to the background fabric, may be used to weave floats on which embroidery stitches can be based. An example is shown in Figure 3-31.

TWILL

In certain cases, the structure of a float weave can be utilized in making up elements of embroidery stitches, by the insertion of colored pattern threads into the weft or warp or both of the fabric structure at the appropriate locations.

Twill weave can be used in this way for many of the embroidery stitches based on the single running stitch (Figure 5-15). Since the selected colored threads are actually part of the weave (rather than supplementary), the overall fabric weight is lighter

FIGURE 5-15. *Embroidery over colored floats in twill weave. (a) selected colored floats in fabric structure; (b) interlaced running stitch.*

FIGURE 5-16. *Detail of sampler showing embroidered stitches over colored threads inserted into twill fabric. From top: wire-fence filling with diamond cross stitches, threaded running stitch designs, interlaced running stitch, interlaced running stitch design, and threaded running stitch design.*

A.

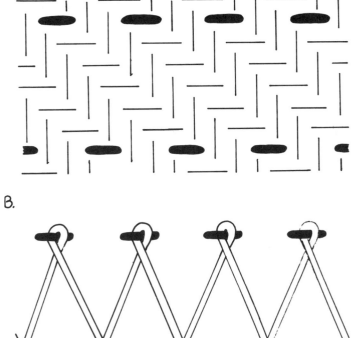

B.

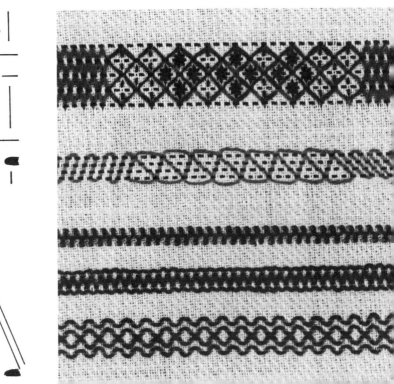

than a similar pattern on a monk's belt type threading. Because twill floats are not usually longer than three threads, they lend themselves best to small-scale patterns. Longer floats, of course, would occur on a relatively coarse twill, woven of heavy thread.

Figure 5-16 shows a portion of a sampler of embroidery stitches based on the floats in a 2/2 twill. Linear patterns such as these can be designed to run vertically as well as horizontally; warp-wise floats as well as weft-wise floats can be woven in a color contrasting with that of the background. Thus, a border pattern of such stitches as whipped, threaded, or interlaced running stitch (as shown in Figures 5-13 and 5-14) could be woven into a twill, using only four harnesses.

Embroidery Stitches for Overall Designs

Figures 5-17 through 5-20 illustrate embroidery stitches that are particularly appropriate for covering broad areas of fabric. On the left side of each sampler are the elements of the stitches that can be woven along with the background fabric; on the right are the completed stitches.

Stitches in the first sampler are based on floats running in one direction only (warp-wise or weft-wise), whereas the remainder incorporate both vertical and horizontal floats.

The top design in Figure 5-17 is an example of couching. Such couched designs, in which various fancy stitches are used to fix long floats onto the background fabric, can be worked over either horizontal or vertical floats, though only horizontal ones are shown here. These long floats can be overlaid on the background fabric either by weaver-controlled pickup or by means of a loom-controlled threading.

Stitches that can be worked over long floats as detached fillings (stitches separate from the background fabric) include chevron stemstitch, raised

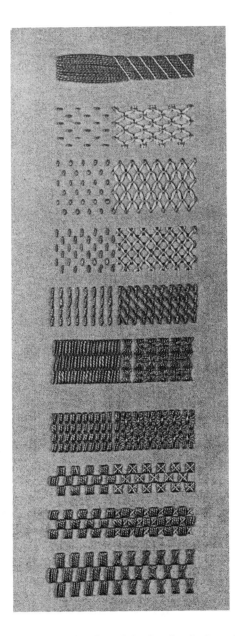

FIGURE 5-17. *Embroidery stitches based on horizontal or vertical floats. From top:* couching with stemstitch, wire-fence filling (I), cloud filling, wire-fence filling (II), Bosnian filling, shellstitch filling, raised double cross stitch, chessboard filling, brick-and-cross filling, *and* staggered sheaf filling.

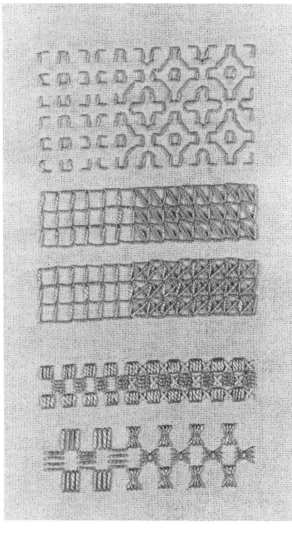

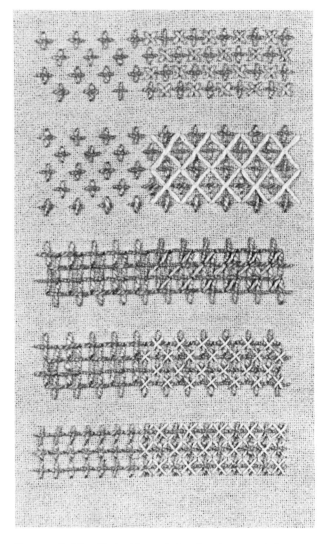

FIGURE 5-18. *Embroidery stitches based on uncrossed vertical and horizontal floats.* From top: *Holbein-work design (one of many possibilities), Turkish filling stitch, two-sided Italian cross stitch, brick-and-cross filling, and Checkerboard sheaf filling.*

FIGURE 5-19. *Embroidery stitches based on straight cross stitch.* From top: *St. George and St. Andrew; large cross with straight cross, diagonal barred-cross filling, double straight-cross filling, and reversed double cross-stitch filling.*

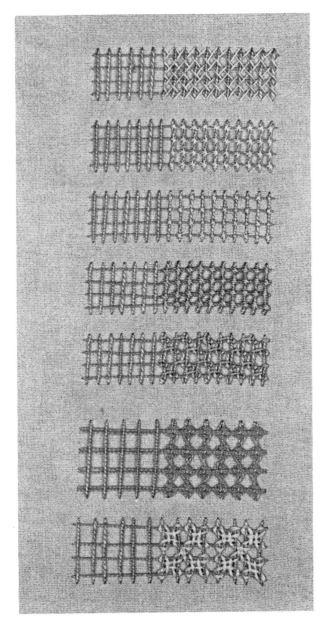

FIGURE 5-20. *Embroidery stitches worked over spaced, crossed floats. From top:* honeycomb lattice filling, raised-honeycomb filling, square couched filling (one of many possible designs), twisted lattice filling, laced lattice filling, double bars with woven-circle filling, *and* Maltese-cross filling.

chain-band filling, Cretan open filling, and various other needle-lace stitches (see Chapter 4 for examples). In these detached filling stitches, the floats act as warp threads.

The remainder of the stitches in Figure 5-17 are based on the single running stitch, with rows of running stitch either evenly spaced or grouped together. Most of the stitches incorporating grouped floats may properly be worked with either vertical or horizontal floats, though primarily vertical floats are shown in the sampler. Weaves appropriate for these stitches include loom-controlled supplementary floats, twill, or other float weaves.

The bidirectional floats over which the stitches in Figures 5-18, 5-19 and 5-20 are worked are either uncrossed or crossed. Shown at the top of Figure 5-18 are stitches based on evenly spaced uncrossed floats. The example of Holbein work, of course, is only one of many possible designs. At the bottom are two stitches based on grouped floats, which are clearly related to two of the grouped-float stitches in Figure 5-17. The only difference is that here floats run both horizontally and vertically.

Straight cross stitch is the basis for stitches in Figure 5-19; many are related to the stitches in Figure 5-6, but have been put together to form overall patterns rather than linear ones.

In Figure 5-20, the stitches are based on grids of long, crossed, widely spaced floats, either detached from the background fabric or sewn down to it. Many design variations are possible with the sewn down type, known generally as square couched fillings; only one is illustrated here. Double weave or, if a multiharness loom is available, a bidirectional monk's belt type threading may be used to weave the floats on which the stitches in Figure 5-20 are based. Alternatively, floats can be woven in one direction only, with the perpendicular floats being embroidered or inlaid in a picked-up shed.

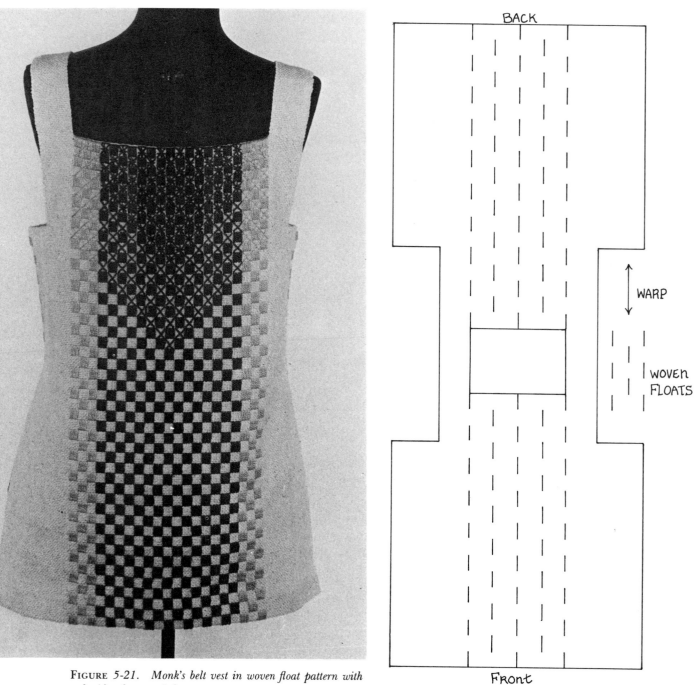

FIGURE 5-21. *Monk's belt vest in woven float pattern with embroidered cross stitches.*

FIGURE 5-22. *Layout of monk's belt vest.*

BACK

WARP

WOVEN FLOATS

Front

Woven Structures for Overall Designs

WEAVER-CONTROLLED PICKUP

If designed to run weft-wise, the long floats required for couching (shown in Figure 5-17) may be set into the woven fabric in a picked-up shed. If only one or a few groups of such floats are needed across the width of the fabric, using the picked-up shed is no slower than embroidering the floats or weaving them on a loom-controlled threading.

Although it is possible to weave stitches based on running stitch in a picked-up shed, use of a loom-controlled threading is much more efficient.

LOOM-CONTROLLED UNIDIRECTIONAL SUPPLEMENTARY FLOATS

All of the stitches in Figure 5-17 may be constructed over supplementary woven floats (see drafts in Figures 5-7, 5-9 and 5-10) on either plain weave, basket weave, or similar woven structures.

An example of such a design is the cotton vest woven in a simple checkerboard pattern on a warp-wise monk's belt threading (Figures 5-21 and C-23). Part of the woven pattern is embellished with cross stitches to form the traditional brick-and-cross embroidery pattern. Threading in the pattern area was the same as for the grouped threads in Figure 5-9, but with a block of six pattern threads instead of

four. The garment, made of 3/2 cotton, was woven to shape (Figure 5-22), and embroidery was done on the loom.

A specialized use for weft-wise or warp-wise supplementary floats is to set in the threads used to draw up gathers for smocking. This can be considerably faster than counting threads or following patterns drawn on the fabric for putting in running stitches by hand, since many rows of precisely positioned gathering threads are required (Figure 5-23a).

Woven stripes, checks, or inlaid patterns can also be planned to coordinate with the smocked design of the finished item (Figure 5-23b).

TWILL

Twill floats can be used as the basis for overall embroidered designs as well as for linear designs. Embroidery stitches that incorporate evenly spaced, small-sized running stitches, such as wire-fence filling and cloud filling, are best suited to the twill structure.

HUCKABACK

Float weaves with grouped floats, such as huckaback, can also be used in some cases as the basis for embroidered fillings, by weaving these floats in a color that sets them off from the rest of the threads. Figure 5-24 includes a small sample of huck incor-

FIGURE 5-23 a and b. Smocking. (a) woven supplementary threads, used to gather the material; (b) woven striped design coordinated with embroidered smocking design.

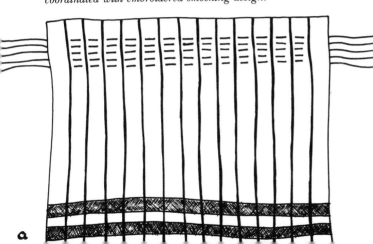

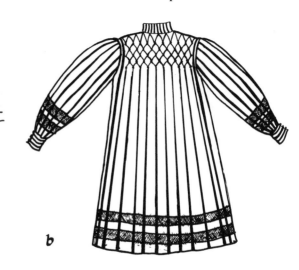

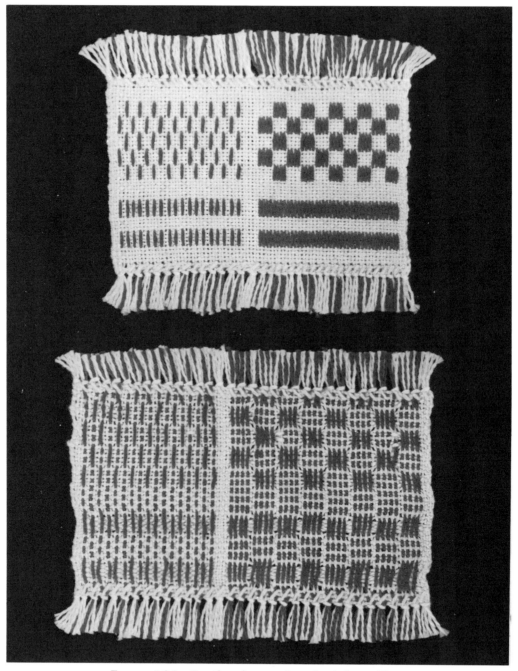

FIGURE 5-24. *Samples of warp-wise colored floats.* Top: *monk's belt (see draft in Figure 5-9);* Bottom: *huckaback.*

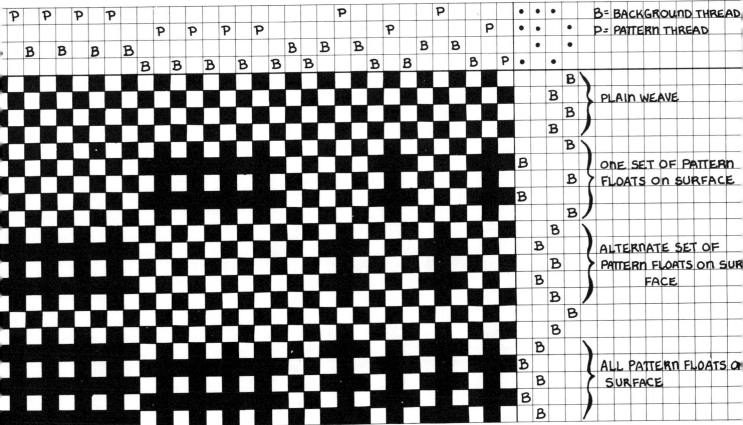

FIGURE 5-25. *Draft for huckaback weave with grouped and spaced colored floats.*

porating colored floats, which has been threaded and treadled to give the same groupings of floats as on the monk's belt sample shown with it. The draft is given in Figure 5-25.

The two weaves look obviously different. The pattern blocks of the monk's belt appear clear cut and the huckaback fabric appears shaded in half tones. In huck fabrics, of course, the float threads also serve as part of the background, so if colored floats are used they show up in the plain weave between floats as well as in the floats themselves.

The usual threading and treadling of a huckaback weave gives a checkerboard of alternating groups of floats. Such a structure could be used as the basis for stitches such as brick-and-cross filling. Since huck can be treadled to give vertical or horizontal floats, the grouped-float stitches in Figure 5-18, as well as those in Figure 5-17, can be worked

on a huckaback threading.

Like twill, huck gives a lighter fabric than a similar monk's belt structure. The latter generally has more total threads per inch (background plus pattern), as the floats are additional to the background rather than incorporated into it.

DOUBLE WEAVE

All of the stitches in Figure 5-20 and some in Figure 5-19 can be woven on a double-weave threading, with the upper surface consisting of threads that are widely spaced and usually heavier than those making up the lower (background) surface (see Figure 3-51, top). For instance, a double-weave grid consisting of pattern threads four background threads apart could be threaded as shown in Figure 5-26. These double-woven floats can be

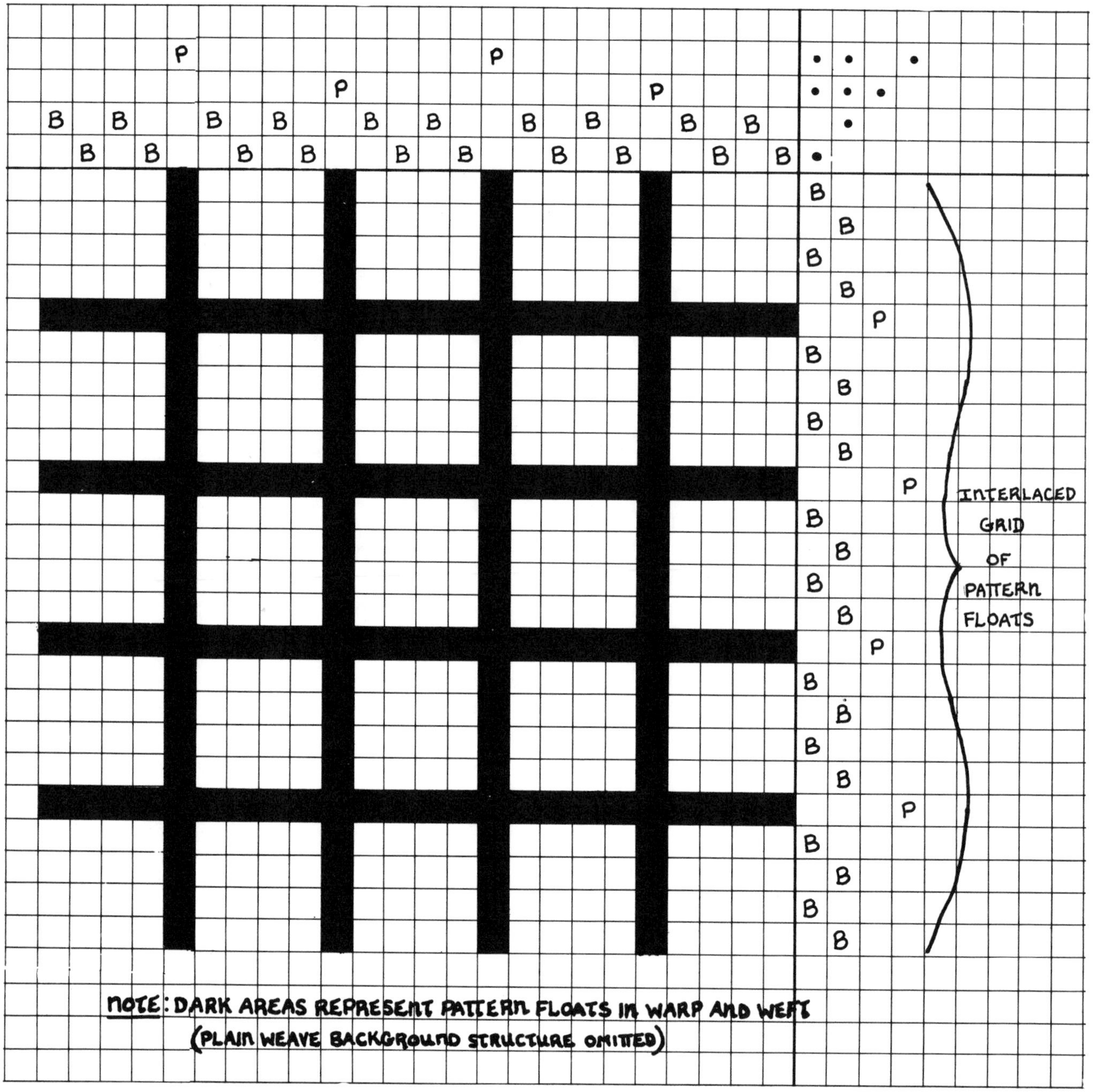

FIGURE 5-26. *Draft for double weave with one surface widely-spaced.*

brought to the surface either as loom-controlled stripes or blocks or as picked-up patterns, as described in Chapter 3.

Some of the stitches shown in Figure 5-20 require an interwoven grid—that is, a true double-woven structure—while some do not. To make an unwoven grid, weft threads are merely laid over the warp threads of the upper surface of the double weave. (Technically, this would be a supplementary warp threading, with weaver-controlled overlaid weft threads.).

Square couched fillings, which are tied down to the background fabric at every corner of the grid, may be interwoven or not. Figure 5-27 shows a sampler of several of these fillings, worked with overlaid wefts rather than a true double-woven structure. The long pattern floats on the reverse side are messy and impractical. A double-weave pickup design would have given a much neater sampler.

A neat reverse side and a great saving of time can be achieved by working couched filling designs over a grid of bidirectional double running stitches. This option, which is available only to weavers with multiharness looms, is drafted, described, and illustrated in the following section.

FIGURE 5-27. *Sampler of couched filling designs over crossed woven floats.*

LOOM-CONTROLLED BIDIRECTIONAL SUPPLEMENTARY FLOATS

Uncrossed bidirectional floats, such as those required for the stitches in Figure 5-18, are most easily woven on a multiharness loom. At least five harnesses are required to produce loom-controlled supplementary floats running both weft-wise and warp-wise. Such a setup can be understood easily if it is thought of as a combination of weft-wise and warp-wise monk's belt.

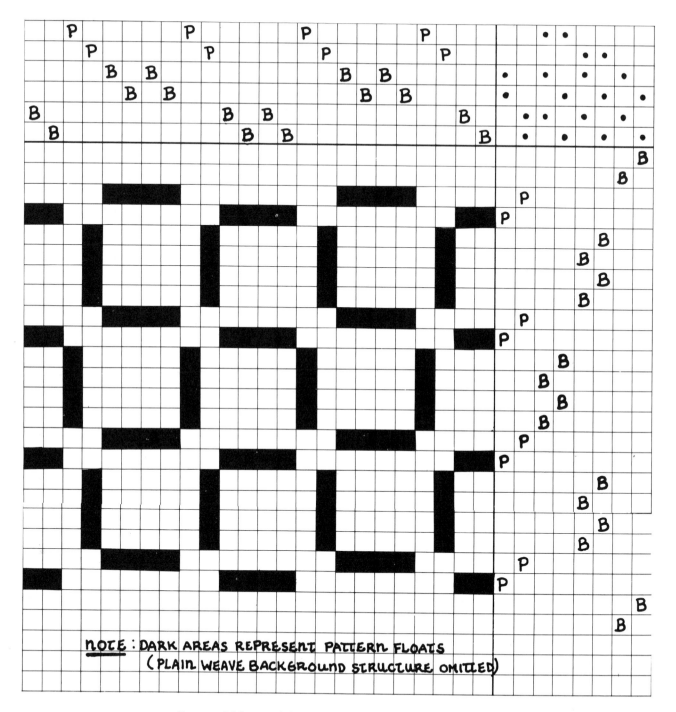

NOTE: DARK AREAS REPRESENT PATTERN FLOATS
(PLAIN WEAVE BACKGROUND STRUCTURE OMITTED)

FIGURE 5-28. *Draft for uncrossed warp-wise and weft-wise supplementary floats over plain weave.*

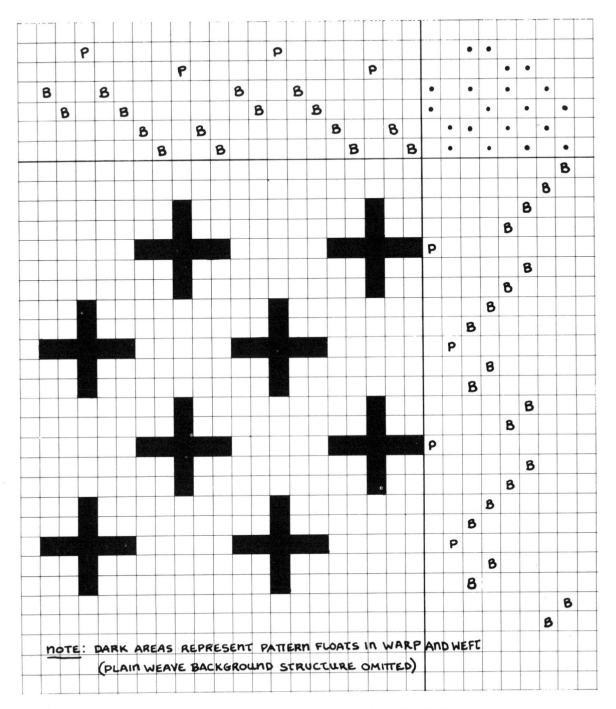

FIGURE 5-29. *Draft for crossed warp-wise and weft-wise supplementary floats over plain weave.*

For instance, to produce the two-sided Italian cross stitch shown in Figure 5-18, the draft given in Figure 5-28 could be used. The first four harnesses are used to control the weft-wise floats, which are laid in as a double running-stitch pattern, while the fifth and sixth harnesses hold the warp-wise pattern floats, which also are treadled to form double running stitches. Into the boxes thus formed, crosses are embroidered to complete the stitch.

A similar combination of vertical and horizontal floats can be devised to give crossed warp and weft threads, as for stitches based on the straight cross stitch. Simply place a pattern warp thread at the center of a weft-float block, rather than at the ends of it, as drafted in Figure 5-29.

The tote bag illustrated in Figure 5-30 uses the draft in Figure 5-28 as the basis for a design derived from square couched fillings. After the basic grid was woven, long diagonal floats tied down by short diagonal stitches were used to complete the design. The handbag in Figure C-2 utilizes a similar pattern of floats on a smaller scale, together with several crewel embroidery stitches.

The advantage in not using a double-weave structure as the basis for these designs is that stitching down the corners of the grid becomes unnecessary, resulting in a considerable saving of time. The overall design, however, is much more limited than double-weave pickup patterns. Another disadvantage is the slight unevenness of the boxes caused by the float structure. The unevenness, however, is covered up by the diagonal floats over much of the design area.

Still another possible way to weave grids for couched-filling designs is to use a structure similar to that produced by Moorman technique, "couching" long supplementary floats to a background fabric by means of additional supplementary woven threads (see Figure 3-31). Bidirectional floats could

FIGURE 5-30. *Tote bag woven with bidirectional supplementary floats and embroidered with couched-filling design.*

certainly be "couched" in the same way as unidirectional floats.

It is an axiom in weaving that whatever technique one considers, the Peruvians probably already tried it. This is certainly true of bidirectional supplementary floats. In *Peru: Textiles Unlimited, Part II* (see Bibliography), Harriet Tidball includes a section on "Supplementary Warp and Weft Outlines" where she gives drafts utilizing six, eight, and eleven harnesses to produce designs similar to Holbein work entirely on the loom (Figure 5-31).

More complex designs similar to Holbein work can be achieved if loom-produced horizontal and vertical pattern elements are supplemented with embroidered diagonal lines. Some possibilities are sketched in Figure 5-32.

In a nutshell, four harnesses are required for the first one or two weft-wise lines of (alternating) floats (as drafted in Figures 5-7 and 5-28), two or four harnesses (depending on the exact placement of the floats relative to each other) for each additional different weft-wise line of pseudo-running stitch, and one harness for each different warp-wise line of floats.

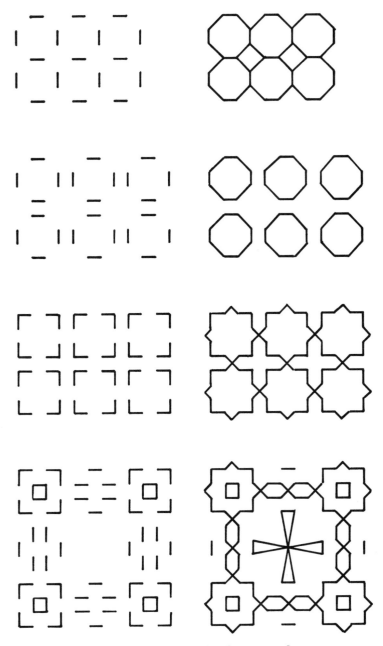

FIGURE 5-32. *Holbein-work designs based on woven floats. Top three designs require five harnesses; bottom design requires eight.*

FIGURE 5-31. *Peruvian woven design using supplementary floats.*

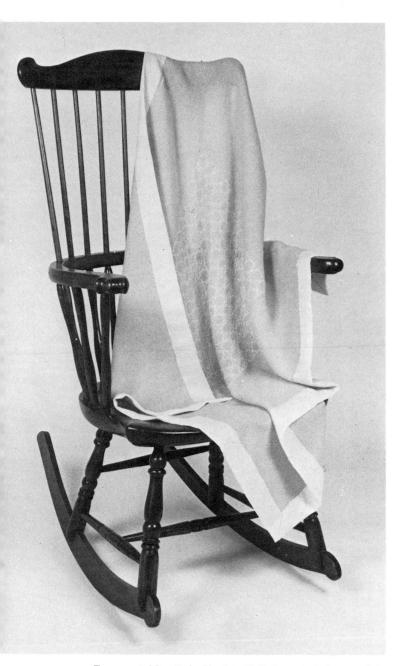

FIGURE 5-33. *Baby blanket. Holbein-work design on plain weave, with warp- and weft-wise woven supplementary floats and diagonal embroidered lines.*

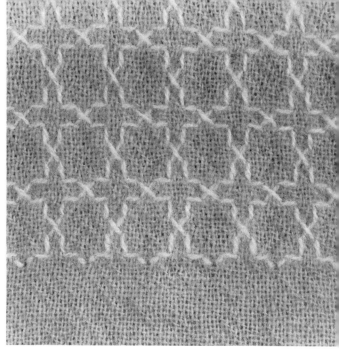

FIGURE 5-34. *Detail of baby blanket.*

The baby blanket shown in Figures 5-33 and C-24 used the third pattern from the top in Figure 5-32. The long ends of the pattern warp threads were used to embroider the diagonal lines of the design (Figure 5-34). The pattern which shows on the reverse side of the blanket is the second from the top in Figure 5-32.

Embroidery books in which blackwork is discussed (see Bibliography) may act as a reservoir of design ideas for this type of combined weaving and embroidery. After horizontal or vertical floats or both have been set in, the addition of diagonal floats proceeds rapidly. Time expenditure is necessary, however, for careful planning of the weaving drafts.

For stitches that use bidirectional grouped threads as part of the design, a draft such as that in Figure 5-35 can be used. The resulting woven design can be embellished with cross stitches or other embroidery.

Other treadling sequences or threading sequences will give different designs—the possibilities are almost endless.

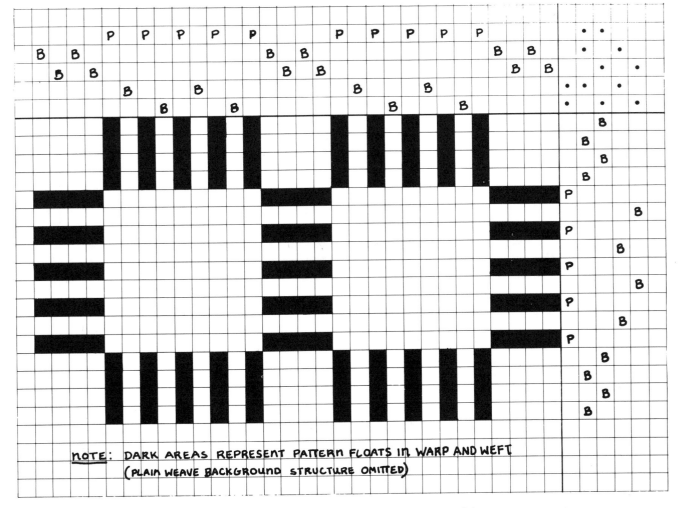

FIGURE 5-35. *Draft for grouped bidirectional floats over plain weave.*

Summary of Structural Relationships between Stitches and Weaves

The outline included at the end of the book should aid the weaver in choosing among embroidery stitches for a given project and in deciding how best to utilize the loom in producing the chosen stitchery design. In the outline, the stitches are organized according to the structure of the floats that form the basis for each stitch. There is a key to indicate which weave or weaves may be used to produce a given stitch. Both *preferred* and *alternative* woven structures have been included.

Designing Embroidery Patterns Based on Woven Floats

Now that we have discussed the means by which portions of embroidery stitches may be produced on the loom, the question may still remain: Why do it? Certainly, these techniques should not be used just for the sake of doing something different—or of doing the same old thing in a different way. I can conceive of only two good justifications for choosing a given method to produce a design: Either it will result in a special effect unobtainable in any other way; or it will result in a significant savings of time or effort. The question, then, is mainly whether time-saving or effort-saving is possible, since all of the designs presented in this chapter can be produced either by embroidery alone or by embroidery plus weaving.

In determining whether to weave or to embroider a given design, one consideration is size. Usually a small, isolated motif is more easily embroidered than woven, whereas a large-scale design may be more suitable for weaving. Setting up the pattern on the loom takes a significant amount of time, which is worth it only if you get the time back some other way.

The designs on the baby blanket (Figure 5-34) and the jacket (Figures 5-13 and 5-14) certainly could have been embroidered entirely by hand. So could an overshot coverlet, but what embroiderer would wish to tackle such a chore?

In weaving portions of embroidery stitches, another consideration, if time is of the essence, is the choice of stitch. Generally, threaded or detached stitches, in which the needle does not pierce the fabric, work up most quickly. Large-scale stitches in heavier threads are naturally faster to embroider than if the same area is covered with much smaller stitches.

You should be aware, of course, that the appearance of embroidery stitches can be varied greatly by choice of thread (thick or thin, dark or light color, etc.) and of size and spacing of floats. Experimentation helps greatly when planning designs.

Since dull, repetitive woven floats can be made to look much more interesting with the addition of only a small amount of needlework, a large area of woven pattern can be embellished only in some sections in order to cut embroidery time to a minimum. The bags in Figures C-2 and 5-30 and the vest in Figures 5-21 and C-23 are examples of this technique. Without the embroidered cross stitches, the tunic design would have been okay, but

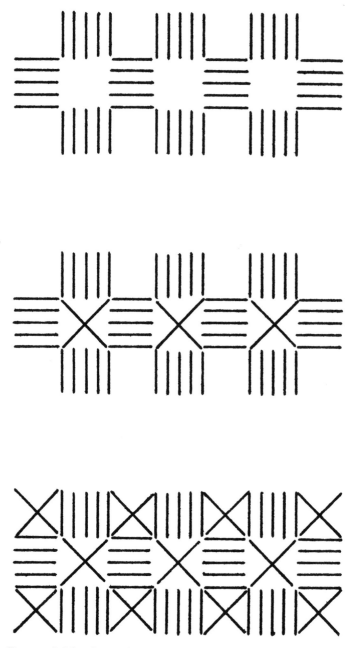

FIGURE 5-36. *Grouped float designs, with embroidered cross stitches.*

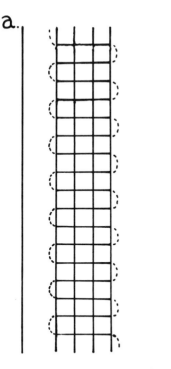
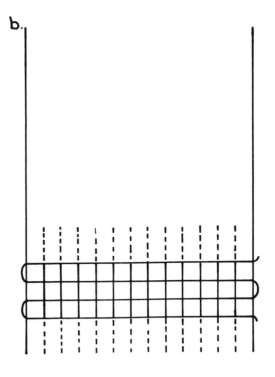

FIGURE 5-37. *Setting up linear designs incorporating bidirectional woven floats: (a) warp-wise–preferred method; (b) weft-wise–unused warp ends are wasted.*

rather dull. With the addition of only a small amount of stitchery, a unique design is achieved. The middle design in Figure 5-36 is more interesting than the top one, but there is no need to use embroidery to fill up every space in the woven design. The bottom pattern, where this has been done, is probably less interesting than either of the others!

Once a design is chosen, the next step is to devise the best way to weave it. In setting up a given pattern on the loom, a weaver will take into consideration the limitations of the loom—width, number of harnesses, etc.—plus his or her own preferences for treadling and weaving. For instance, whether to use warp-wise or weft-wise supplementary threads may be determined by whether the preference is to use one shuttle or two.

In the case of border designs incorporating bidirectional floats, where the pattern does not cover the entire surface of the fabric, it is usually best to try to set up the design so that it runs warp-wise on the fabric (Figure 5-37). This way, the weft floats can be inlaid to cover only the patterned area. If such a pattern were set up weft-wise, all the warp ends of the floats would have to be cut and tied off or otherwise disposed of. Aside from the inconvenience involved, this results in a waste of the pattern thread.

As discussed in Chapter 2, fiber content and fabric finishing processes must also be taken into account, ideally in the earliest stages of planning and designing a given article. These considerations will be instrumental in deciding, for instance, whether to complete embroidery while the item is on the loom or wait until after washing and pressing it.

Summary Outline: Embroidery over Unwoven Warp or Weft Threads (CHAPTER 4)

| | Appearance | | |
	Opaque	Lacy	*Related to traditional woven structure*
I. Linear designs			
A. Perpendicular to warp threads			
1. Drawn-thread embroidery			
a. Hemstitch			
i. Ladder		x	
ii. Sawtooth		x	
b. Crossed groups		x	Gauze, leno
c. Knotted groups		x	Leno, Brooks bouquet
d. Sheafstitch		x	Brooks bouquet
e. Corded or buttonholed groups		x	Wrapping
f. Webs		x	Plain weave, Egyptian knot
g. Needleweaving	x	x	Plain weave
h. Single featherstitch	x	x	
2. Band stitches			
a. Stemstitch band	x	x	Soumak
b. Portuguese border stitch	x	x	Soumak
c. Lockstitch	x	x	Soumak, Ghiordes knot
d. Double lockstitch (cablestitch)	x	x	Soumak
e. Raised stem band	x	x	Egyptian knot
f. Raised buttonhole	x	x	
g. Cretan open filling		x	
h. Woven band stitches	x		Twining
i. Checkered chain band	x		Twining
j. Raised chain band	x	x	
3. Chain stitch	x		Weft chaining
4. Twisted chain stitch	x	x	
5. Soumak			Soumak
a. Wrapped	x	x	
b. Looped	x	x	
c. Buttonholed	x	x	
6. Needle lace			
a. Ceylon (loop) stitch	x	x	
B. Parallel to warp threads (between two or more warps)			
1. Ladder stitch	x	x	
2. Vandyke stitch	x		
3. Cretan stitch	x	x	
4. Chevron stemstitch	x	x	Soumak
5. Needle-lace stitches (See II.A.2.)			

	Appearance		
---	Opaque	Lacy	Related to traditional woven structure
II. Overall designs			
A. Needle-lace fillings			
1. Worked perpendicular to warp			
a. Ceylon (loop) stitch	x	x	
2. Worked parallel to warp			
a. Detached buttonhole	x	x	
b. Spaced buttonhole		x	
c. Detached up-and-down buttonhole	x	x	
d. Knotted buttonhole	x	x	
e. Knotted double buttonhole		x	
f. Venetian point		x	
g. Valsesian stitch	x	x	
h. Hollie stitch	x	x	
i. Tulle stitch		x	
j. Diamond filling		x	Plain weave
B. Detached fillings			
1. Russian overcast	x		
2. Raised honeycomb	x		
3. Honeycomb	x	x	
4. Twisted lattice		x	
5. Laced lattice	x	x	
6. Double bars with woven circle		x	
7. Maltese cross		x	
C. Needleweaving	x	x	Plain weave
D. Band stitches			
1. Cretan open filling		x	
2. Woven band stitches	x		Twining
3. Chevron stemstitch	x	x	Soumak
E. Soumak variations (See I.A.5.)	x	x	Soumak
F. Chain-stitch variations (See I.A.)	x	x	Weft chaining

Summary Outline: Embroidery Stitches and Techniques for Use on Woven Floats (CHAPTER 5)

Float Structure	Stitch	1	2	3	Twill	Huck	Double Weave
I. Linear designs							
A. Unidirectional floats (vertical or horizontal)							
1. Floats parallel to linear direction							
a. Single (long) floats							
i. Solitary	Couching/laid work	X	x				
	Thorn stitch	X	x				
ii. Grouped	Buttonholed bar	X	x				
	Chained bar	X	x				
	Chevron stemstitch	X	x				
b. Dashed line	Single running stitch	x	X			x	
i. Solitary line	Double threaded (laced) running stitch	x	X			x	
	Double whipped running stitch	x	X			x	
	Threaded (laced) running stitch	x	X			x	
	Whipped running stitch	x	X			x	
ii. Paired lines							
(a) Unseparated	Dot stitch	x	X				
	Double threaded (laced) running stitch	x	X				
	Double whipped running stitch	x	X				
	Threaded (laced) running stitch	x	X				
	Whipped running stitch	x	X				
(b) Separated							
(i) Parallel floats	Double back-laced running stitch	x	X			x	
	Holbein-work designs	x	X			x	
(ii) Staggered floats	Interlaced running stitch	x	X			x	
	Holbein-work designs	x	X			x	
iii. Multiple lines (unseparated)	Brick and cross (one row)	x	X				
	Guilloche stitch	x	X				
c. "Solid" line	Double running stitch	x	X				
i. Solitary line	Double threaded (laced) double running stitch	x	X				
	Double whipped double running stitch	x	X				
	Pekinese stitch	x	X				
	Threaded (laced) double running stitch	x	X				
	Whipped double running (overcast) stitch	x	X				

Float Structure	Stitch	Supplementary Floats 1	2	3	Twill	Huck	Double Weave
ii. Paired lines (separated)							
(a) Parallel ‑ ‑ ‑ ‑ ‑	Double Pekinese stitch	x	X				
‑ ‑ ‑ ‑ ‑	Raised Cretan stitch	x	X				
(b) Staggered ▬▬▬▬▬	Interlaced band	x	X				
2. Floats perpendicular to linear direction							
a. Evenly spaced floats ▬ ▬ ▬ ▬	Bosnian stitch	x	X				
| | | | | |	Checkered chain band	x	X				
	Cross stitch with bar	x	X				
	Drawn-thread embroidery designs	x	X				
	Double lock (cable) stitch	x	X				
	Lockstitch	x	X				
	Needleweaving	x	X				
	Portuguese border stitch	x	X				
	Raised buttonhole stitch	x	X				
	Raised chain band stitch	x	X				
	Shellstitch	x	X				
	Stemstitch band	x	X				
	Triangle stitch	x	X				
b. Paired floats || || || ||	Woven band stitches	x	X				
	Zigzag stitch	x	X				
c. Multigrouped floats ||| ||| |||	Chained butterfly stitch	x	X				
	Sheafstitch	x	X				
B. Bidirectional floats (vertical *and* horizontal)							
1. Uncrossed ☐ ☐ ☐	Holbein-work designs	x	x	X			
2. Crossed + + +	Diamond cross stitch	x	X	X			x
	Oriental cross stitch	x	X	X			x
	Reversed double cross stitch	x	X	X			x
	St. George and St. Andrew	x	X	X			x
	Straight cross stitch	x	X	X			x
II. Overall designs							
A. Uni-directional floats							
1. Long floats							
a. Evenly spaced							
i. Horizontal ≡≡≡	Chevron stemstitch	X	X				
	Needle-lace stitches	X	X				
	Raised chain band filling	X	X				
ii. Vertical ||||||||	Ceylon (loop) stitch	X	X				
	Cretan open filling	X	X				

Summary Outline: Embroidery Stitches and Techniques for Use on Woven Floats (CHAPTER 5)

Float Structure	Stitch	Supplementary Floats 1	2	3	Twill	Huck	Double Weave
b. Solidly placed (vertical or horizontal)	Couching	X	X				
	Surface satinstitch	X	X				
2. Dashed lines							
a. Evenly spaced							
i. Horizontal	Gathering stitches for smocking	x	X				
	Wire fence filling	x	X			x	
	Bosnian filling	x	X				
ii. Vertical	Cloud filling	x	X			x	
	Wire fence filling (var.)	x	X			x	
	Shellstitch filling	x	X				
b. Grouped (vertical or horizontal)							
i. Parallel groups	Raised cross stitch	x	X				
	Raised double cross stitch	x	X				
	Raised rice stitch	x	X				
ii. Staggered groups	Brick-and-cross filling	x	X			x	
	Checkerboard filling	x	X			x	
	Chessboard filling	x	X			x	
	Staggered sheaf filling	x	X				
B. Bidirectional floats							
1. Uncrossed							
a. Evenly spaced	Holbein-work designs	x	x	X			
	Turkish filling stitch	x	x	X			
	Two-sided Italian cross stitch	x	x	X			
b. Grouped	Brick-and-cross filling		x	X		x	
	Checkerboard sheaf filling		x	X			
2. Crossed							
a. Short	Diagonal barred cross filling		x	X			x
	Diamond cross stitch		x	X			x
	Double cross stitch filling		x	X			x
	Large cross with straight cross		x	X			x
	Reversed double cross stitch		x	X			x
	St. George and St. Andrew		x	X			x
	Straight cross stitch		x	X			x
	Star filling		x	X			x
b. Long							
i. Evenly spaced							
(a) Not interwoven							
(i) Detached from background	Double whipped detached filling	X---X					
	Honeycomb fillings	X---X					
	Raised honeycomb filling	X---X					
	Russian overcast filling	X---X					

Float Structure	Stitch	Supplementary Floats			Twill	Huck	Double Weave
		1	*2*	*3*			
(ii) Fixed to background	Square couched fillings	X---X			X		
(b) Interwoven	Laced lattice filling						X
	Twisted lattice filling						X
	Woven ground fillings						X
ii. Grouped							
(a) Not interwoven							
(i) Detached from background	Double bars with woven circle filling	X---X					
(ii) Fixed to background	Waffle filling	X---X					x
(b) Interwoven (detached)	Drawn-thread embroidery fillings						X
	Maltese cross filling						X

KEY
    1 = Weaver-controlled pickup (weft-wise)
    2 = Warp-wise or weft-wise floats, loom-controlled
    3 = Warp-wise and weft-wise floats, loom-controlled
    X = Preferred woven structure
    x = Other possible weaving method(s)
X---X
    = Combination of two weaving methods
x---x

Glossary

ASSISI WORK. A counted-thread embroidery technique in which design motifs are outlined in a double running stitch or back stitch, then left blank while the background is filled in with cross stitch.

BALANCED WEAVE. Weave in which there are the same number of warp threads per inch as weft threads.

BAND STITCH. Linear embroidery stitch worked over embroidered floats rather than directly into the background fabric.

BARGELLO WORK. See Florentine embroidery.

BASKET WEAVE. Balanced plain weave with multiple warps and wefts. Monk's cloth is a basket-weave fabric with quadruple warps and wefts.

BLACKWORK EMBROIDERY. See Holbein work.

BLOCK OR UNIT WEAVE. Loom-controlled weave in which designs may be built up by the combination of rectangular pattern areas.

BOUND WEAVE. Weft-faced weave in two or more colors, woven on a pattern threading (twill, overshot, etc.). Design is formed by combination of treadling sequence and weft color sequence.

BROCADE DESIGN. Usually refers to woven patterns produced by supplementary weft threads which do not run from selvedge to selvedge.

BROOKS BOUQUET. One of a number of weaver-controlled weaves in which weft wraps around and constricts groups of warp threads.

CANVAS WEAVE. A basketlike balanced float weave, often constructed with regularly spaced holes.

CANVAS EMBROIDERY (NEEDLEPOINT). A type ·of counted-thread embroidery in which the embroidery thread completely covers the background fabric. Tra-

ditionally, but not necessarily, worked on a stiff backing with widely-spaced warp and weft.

CORDUROY. Loom-controlled weft-pile fabric, in which the pile is produced by cutting long woven floats. Technique used for rugs, as well as for lighter fabrics.

COUCHING, OR LAIDWORK. Embroidery technique which uses counted-thread stitches to tie down long threads laid on top of the fabric. It is often used with metal threads, in order not to waste any of the precious material on the back side of the fabric. Couched fillings usually are built up from grids of threads laid perpendicular to each other.

COUNTED-THREAD EMBROIDERY. Embroidery technique in which stitches are worked over a specific number of threads, preferably on a balanced (even-weave) fabric. The stitches do not necessarily completely cover the background. (These same stitches may also be used in free embroidery, over any number of threads, on almost any fabric.)

CRACKLE WEAVE. Block weave using a supplementary pattern weft on a tabby background. Pattern blocks are made up of short floats and form overlapping designs.

CREWEL EMBROIDERY. A rather loose term, designating a type of embroidery, usually in wool, which uses such stitches as stem, chain, and satin to fill in designs (often floral) on an unembroidered background fabric.

DETACHED FILLINGS. Embroidered designs based on grids or parallel groups of long threads. The grid may be decorated by interweaving in various ways, but is not tied down to the background fabric except at the edges of the design.

DOUBLE CLOTH. Fabric composed of two separate sets

of warps and wefts, forming two layers of cloth which may be interchanged to bring one or the other layer to the upper surface of the fabric.

DOUBLE WEAVE. Weave composed of two complete weave structures.

DOUBLE WEAVE PICKUP. Weaver-controlled method of forming designs on a double-woven fabric by interchanging the two woven surfaces; the pattern on one side is the reverse of that on the other.

DRAWN-THREAD EMBROIDERY. Embroidery technique traditionally worked over a tabby fabric from which threads have been withdrawn in either one direction or two. The resulting spaces are secured along the edges, then the empty warp or weft threads are embellished by various stitchery techniques.

EGYPTIAN KNOT. Wrapped woven structure equivalent to the reverse side of some soumak structures. Worked from "right" side of fabric.

EMBROIDERY WEAVE. May be used as a synonym for *brocade*.

EPI. Ends (of warp) per inch.

FLAMEPOINT. See Florentine embroidery.

FLOAT. Portion of a weft (or warp) thread extending unbound over two or more warp (or weft) threads.

FLOAT WEAVE. Weave in which warp or weft floats or both form an organized structure.

FLORENTINE EMBROIDERY. Canvas embroidery technique with characteristic linear, steplike geometric patterns, usually employing several colors grading from light to dark or along the spectrum. Also called Bargello or flamepoint.

GAUZE. Structure in which warp threads are crossed over other warps and secured with a weft before being returned to their original order.

GHIORDES, OR TURKISH, KNOT. Pile structure composed of a supplementary weft symmetrically wrapped around warp threads to form a series of loops, which may or may not be cut. (Cut pile may also be made with separate, short pieces of weft.) One of a number of pile knots used in rug-making.

HALF-TAPESTRY WEAVE. Weave using inlaid pattern threads in a widely-spaced tabby to form designs. Also called transparent weave.

HARDANGER WORK. Norwegian drawn-thread embroidery technique. Traditionally utilizes geometric designs based on withdrawal of threads from a fabric in two directions. The mesh area thus formed is secured around

its edges by blocks of satinstitch, and the open threads in it are often wrapped to give a pronounced grid, then further decorated with other stitches.

HARNESS. Frame that holds heddles; one of the parts of a loom. Used to lift (or lower) warp threads so that weft can be inserted. The more harnesses on a loom, the more (and more complex) loom-controlled patterns can be woven.

HEDDLE STICK. Simple harness device consisting of a stick onto which string heddles are knotted.

HEDDLES. String or metal devices through which individual warp ends are threaded on the loom.

HOLBEIN WORK. Counted-thread embroidery technique, also called blackwork, in which designs are developed almost entirely in double running stitch or backstitch. Traditionally worked in black thread on white or natural colored material.

HUCKABACK. Float weave consisting of groups of floats, or single floats, alternating with plain weave.

HUCK EMBROIDERY. A type of mock weaving, in which decorative colored yarns are threaded through the floats of a huckaback material, producing typical traditional patterns. Most often used as borders on towels.

HV TECHNIQUE. See half-tapestry weave.

INLAID, OR LAID-IN, WEFT. Supplementary weft added in the same shed as the background weft. Term may be used loosely to include overlaid and underlaid wefts.

LENO. Fabric composed of areas of gauze and plain weave.

MOCK WEAVING. Embroidery technique which uses running stitch to form patterns. May closely resemble woven inlaid patterns.

MONK'S BELT. A block weave in which pattern blocks are formed by long floats of supplementary weft or warp on a tabby background.

MOORMAN TECHNIQUE. A type of woven inlay in which thin supplementary warp threads are used to tie supplementary weft pattern threads down to the fabric surface.

NÄVERSÖM WORK. Scandinavian drawn-thread embroidery technique worked over a mesh. Produces design areas within the mesh (rather than producing shaped mesh areas on a plain weave background, as in Hardanger work).

NEEDLE LACE. Lace made with one or two single elements, using needle and thread. Each row is looped or knotted into the previous one.

NEEDLEPOINT.   See canvas embroidery.

NEEDLEWEAVING.   A type of drawn-threadwork in which a needle is used to weave decorative motifs onto the open threads.

OVERLAID WEFT.   Supplementary weft added to form floats on the top side of the fabric.

OVERSHOT WEAVE.   A block weave using supplementary weft floats on a tabby background to form patterns. The pattern thread characteristically produces areas of both long floats and inlaid tabby.

PATTERN DARNING.   A type of mock weaving, in which designs are made up of running stitches of different lengths. May be structurally identical to woven brocade or inlay.

PATTERN WEAVE.   Fancy weave; not plain weave. May be "area-patterned" or "weave-patterned." (See Emery in Bibliography for discussion.)

PICK.   Single shot of weft thread through shed.

PICK-AND-PICK.   Designs formed by the order in which different colored wefts are inserted into a weft-faced weave. Identical effect may be achieved in a warp-faced weave.

PICKUP STICK.   Smooth stick with beveled edges, used to pick up warp threads for certain weaver-controlled pattern weaves.

PILE.   Cut or uncut loops of yarn forming the surface of a fabric.

PLAIN, OR TABBY, WEAVE.   Structure in which weft passes alternately over and under every warp. Balanced plain weave has equally spaced warp and weft elements of approximately the same size.

PULLED-THREAD EMBROIDERY.   A type of counted-thread embroidery in which stitches are pulled very tightly, resulting in a lacy openwork design. Also called pulled fabric or drawn fabric embroidery.

RYA.   Pile technique employing the Ghiordes knot, with rows of knots forming a long pile separated by fairly wide areas of weft-faced weave. Knots may be embroidered on a prewoven backing.

SELVEDGE.   Reinforced warp sides of a fabric. Some fabrics are woven with both weft-wise and warp-wise selvedges.

SETT.   Number of warp threads per inch.

SHADOW PLAID.   Plaid formed by different-sized or differently spaced warps and wefts, as opposed to differently colored threads.

SHADOW WORK.   Embroidery technique using double back stitch to make designs on sheer fabric which appear different depending on whether light shines on them or through them.

SHED.   Opening formed in warp by raising or lowering some threads, through which shuttle is passed.

SICILIAN WORK.   One of many localized embroidery techniques employing a drawn-thread mesh (usually wrapped) as background, with design motifs showing up in plain weave.

SLEY.   Put warp threads through dents in reed, which spaces them.

SMOCKING.   An embroidery technique used to fix an area of gathered or pleated fabric into a rather elastic structure. Often uses counted-thread stitches on top of the pleated fabric as decorative motifs, as well as to hold the pleats.

SOUMAK.   A type of weft wrapping (usually over two or four warp threads, and back under one or two, etc.); in rugs, supplementary to a (usually) plain-weave background. Structure of reverse side equivalent to single soumak, Egyptian knot, Swedish knot, etc., depending on its exact construction.

SPANISH LACE.   Plain-weave structure formed by a weft that moves forward-backward-forward across small groups of warp threads until it progresses completely across the warp.

STUMP WORK.   A three-dimensional type of embroidery, employing needle lace, needleweaving, and various textured embroidery stitches. Designs are often padded for additional relief.

SUMMER-AND-WINTER WEAVE.   A block weave in which a supplementary weft overlays (or underlays) the plain-weave background in floats over (or under) three warp threads.

SUPPLEMENTARY ELEMENTS.   Warp or weft threads or both which are additional to the background structure of the fabric.

TABBY.   See plain weave.

TAPESTRY WEAVE.   Weft-faced weave, with discontinuous wefts forming mosaic-like pattern areas. There may be many color changes across the width of the fabric.

TEMPLE.   Device for keeping the selvedges of a fabric equally spaced as weaving proceeds.

TRANSPARENT WEAVE.   See half-tapestry.

TURKEY WORK.   Embroidery technique employing the structural equivalent of the Ghiordes knot to produce a cut-pile surface on a fabric backing.

TWILL WEAVE. A float weave characterized by the diagonal alignment of floats.

TWINING. Technique consisting of one set of straight threads (warp or weft) enclosed by a pair of threads that twist around each other as they pass alternately over and under successive straight threads.

UNDERLAID WEFT. Supplementary weft added to form floats on the botton side of the fabric.

WAFFLE WEAVE. A balanced float weave in which warp and weft floats form square patterns.

WARP. Logitudinal threads on the loom, into which weft threads are woven.

WARP BEAM. Device at back of loom around which unwoven warp is wound.

WARP-FACED WEAVE. Structure in which warp completely covers weft.

WEFT. Thread woven through and usually perpendicular to the warp. Also called filling or woof.

WEFT CHAINING. A type of weft wrapping in which groups of warp threads are enclosed by a single weft thread looping around them. Same structure as chain stitch, but worked with fingers or crochet hook rather than with needle on pre-woven fabric.

WEFT-FACED WEAVE. Structure in which weft completely covers warp.

Bibliography

Anchor Manual of Needlework. London: B. T. Batsford Ltd., 1970. (499 pp.) An old standby, including many different techniques, such as smocking, counted-thread embroidery, drawn-thread embroidery, Sicilian work, Hardanger work, Assisi work, Holbein work, pulled-thread embroidery, canvas embroidery, needle lace, and more.

Birrell, Verla. *The Textile Arts.* New York: Schocken, 1959. (512 pp.) Essentially an encyclopedia of textile processes, including weaving, embroidery and other techniques. Excellent reference.

Black, Mary E. *New Key to Weaving.* New York: Bruce Publishing, 1957. (573 pp.) Excellent overall weaving book describing plain weaves, inlay, weaver-controlled lace weaves, soumak, knotting, twill, monk's belt, overshot, summer and winter, basket weave, huckaback, waffle weave, tapestry weave, and double weaves, including picked up designs.

Coats & Clark's. *One Hundred Embroidery Stitches.* New York: Coats & Clark's, 1964. (34 pp.) Handy pocket-sized dictionary of stitches describing counted-thread embroidery, drawn-thread embroidery, canvas embroidery, pulled-thread embroidery, and joining stitches.

Collingwood, Peter. *The Techniques of Rug Weaving.* New York: Watson-Guptill, 1968. (527 pp.) Excellent instruction in weft-faced and warp-faced weaves. Includes pick-and-pick, tapestry weaves, soumak, weft chaining, twining, knotting, twill, pick-and-pick, picked-up block weaves, picked-up double weaves, corduroy weave, and rug finishes.

Davison, Marguerite Porter. *A Handweaver's Pattern Book.* Swarthmore, PA: Marguerite P. Davison, Publisher, 1944. (217 pp.) Drafts and illustrations of almost 400 patterns including fancy twills, basket weaves, canvas weaves, huckabacks, monk's belt, summer and winter, and overshot.

D. M. C. *Die Durchbrucharbeit, I. Serie.* Mulhouse, France: Dollfus-Meig & Co. (95 pp.) In German, but with excellent diagrams. Describes drawn-thread embroidery, including hemstitching, needleweaving, and Hardanger work.

D. M. C. *Ricami Diversi.* Milan, Italy: Dollfus-Meig & Co. (20 pp.) Pulled-thread and counted-thread embroidery patterns and stitches.

Emery, Irene. *The Primary Structures of Fabrics.* Washington, DC: The Textile Museum, 1966. (339 pp.) Basic reference for textile terminology and structural relationships.

Enthoven, Jacqueline. *The Stitches of Creative Embroidery.* New York: Van Nostrand Reinhold, 1964. (212 pp.) Excellent source for counted-thread embroidery stitches and patterns, including Holbein work and couched fillings.

Fangel, Esther; Winckler, Ida; and Madsen, Agnete. *Danish Pulled Thread Embroidery.* New York: Dover, 1977. (100 pp.) Republication of *Pulled Thread Work I* and *II.* Copenhagen: Haandarbejdets Fremmes Forlag, 1958. In Danish and English with excellent diagrams. Has 45 pulled-thread stitches and patterns, plus examples of items decorated with pulled-thread embroidery designs.

Frey, Berta. *Designing and Drafting for Handweavers.* New York: Collier, 1958. (225 pp.) Excellent instruction in design and analysis of fabrics, particularly block weaves. Includes picked-up block weaves, summer and winter, and other pattern weaves.

Geddes, Elisabeth, and McNeill, Moyra. *Blackwork Em-*

broidery. New York: Dover, 1976. (115 pp.) Counted-thread embroidery with many designs of the Holbein-work type.

Hoppe, Elisabeth; Ostlund, Estine; and Melen, Lisa. *Free Weaving on Frame and Loom*. New York: Van Nostrand Reinhold, 1972. (90 pp.) Traditional Scandinavian weaving techniques, including picked-up double weave and half tapestry.

Ireys, Katharine. *The Encyclopedia of Canvas Embroidery Stitch Patterns*. New York: Crowell, 1972. (160 pp.) A basic source book for canvas embroidery. Has over 150 stitches and combinations of stitches, with excellent diagrams.

John, Edith. *Filling Stitches*. London: Batsford, 1967. (96 pp.) Includes couched fillings, detached fillings, and canvas embroidery stitches, with many original variations.

King, Bucky. "Weaving as Related to Embroidery." *Shuttle, Spindle & Dyepot*, v. 1, no. 2 (March 1970):6–7. Historical and structural relationships between the two techniques.

Kreig, Mildred V. *Huck Towel Patterns*. Eugene, OR: Mildred V. Kreig, Publisher, 1964. (14 pp.) Has 30 huck embroidery designs.

Lantz, Sherlee. *A Pageant of Pattern for Needlepoint Canvas*. New York: Atheneum, 1973. (509 pp.) An overwhelming number of canvas embroidery patterns, mostly based on historical designs, with large, clear diagrams. Also some pulled-thread embroidery.

McNeill, Moyra. *Pulled-Thread Embroidery*. New York: Taplinger, 1971. (207 pp.) Basic reference for pulled-thread embroidery. Includes over 60 stitches, edging finishes, and clear diagrams and examples.

Melen, Lisa. *Drawn Threadwork*. New York: Van Nostrand Reinhold, 1968. (96 pp.) Näversöm-work stitches and patterns.

Moorman, Theo. *Weaving as an Art Form*. New York: Van Nostrand Reinhold, 1975. (104 pp.) Describes the Moorman Technique.

Neher, Evelyn. *Four-Harness Huck*. Guilford, CT: Evelyn Neher, Publisher, 1953. (40 pp.) Design of huckaback fabrics, with over 100 pattern variations.

Nichols, Marion. *Encyclopedia of Embroidery Stitches, including Crewel*. New York: Dover, 1974. (214 pp.) Good summary of counted-thread stitches, including couching.

Nordfors, Jill. *Needle Lace & Needleweaving*. New York: Van Nostrand Reinhold, 1974. (160 pp.) Excellent reference for the subjects, with over 80 stitches, including joinings and edgings, and clear diagrams.

Pacque, Joan Michaels. *Design Principles and Fiber Techniques*. Shorewood, WI: Joan and Henry Paque, Publishers, 1973. (103 pp.) Notebook format of many different fiber structures, including knotting, needle lace, detached embroidery stitches, soumak, twining, etc. Good diagrams and photos.

Petersen, Grete, and Svennås, Elsie. *Handbook of Stitches*. New York: Van Nostrand Reinhold, 1970. (73 pp.) A fine little book, covering many stitches and techniques, including counted-thread embroidery, edgings, joinings, couched fillings, needle lace, canvas embroidery, pulled-thread embroidery, drawn-thread embroidery, needleweaving, Hardanger work, and smocking.

Regensteiner, Else. *The Art of Weaving*. New York: Van Nostrand Reinhold, 1970. (184 pp.) Various weaving techniques for beginners, such as plain weaves, basket weave, twills, summer and winter, finger-controlled lace weaves, double weaves including picked-up designs, tapestry, and knotting.

Snook, Barbara. *Florentine Embroidery*. New York: Scribner's, 1967. (160 pp.) Has many diagrams of patterns for this type of embroidery.

Svennas, Elsie. *A Handbook of Lettering for Stitchers*. New York: Van Nostrand Reinhold, 1973. (92 pp.) Handy design reference, with over 30 different alphabets, many of which can be reproduced in double weave or block weaves, as well as by embroidery.

Thomas, Mary. *Dictionary of Embroidery Stitches*. New York: Gramercy Publishing, 1935. (234 pp.) Approximately 300 stitches with good diagrams. Includes counted-thread embroidery, canvas embroidery, pulled-thread embroidery, drawn-thread embroidery, edgings and joinings.

——————. *Mary Thomas's Embroidery Book*. New York: Gramercy Publishing, 1936. (304 pp.) Descriptions and examples of 30 embroidery techniques, including some stitches. Describes Assisi work, blackwork, canvas embroidery, couching, Holbein work, pulled-thread embroidery, drawn-thread embroidery, Hardanger work, needleweaving, joinings, edgings, and smocking.

Tidball, Harriet. *Brocade*. Lansing, MI: Shuttle Craft Guild, 1967. (50 pp.) Inlay, including half tapestry, overlay, underlay, pickup.

——————. *The Double Weave, Plain and Patterned*. Lansing, MI: Shuttle Craft Guild, 1960. (34 pp.) All you ever wanted to know about double weave.

——————. *Peru: Textiles Unlimited, Part II*. Lansing,

MI: Shuttle Craft Guild, 1969. (46 pp.) Describes supplementary warp, including picked-up designs, supplementary weft, including picked-up designs, supplementary warp and weft.

—————. *Supplementary Warp Patterning.* Lansing, MI: Shuttle Craft Guild, 1966. (46 pp.) Describes supplementary warp techniques, including distorted threads, picked-up designs and coordinated warp-weft patterns, and adapting single-beam and two-harness looms.

—————. *Two-Harness Textiles: The Open-Work Weaves.* Lansing, MI: Shuttle Craft Guild, 1967. (34 pp.) Interrupted weft weaves, Spanish lace, wrapping, warp bouquets, weft bouquets, gauze, and leno.

—————. *Two-Harness Textiles: The Loom-Controlled Weaves.* Lansing, MI: Shuttle Craft Guild, 1967. (30 pp.) Plain weaves: balanced, weft-faced, warp-faced, spaced structures, stripes, checks and plaids, inlay, basket weave.

West, Virginia. *Finishing Touches for the Handweaver.* Newton, MA: Branford, 1968. (102 pp.) Includes lace weaves, fringes, embroidered hems, and joinings.

Wilson, Erica. *Erica Wilson's Embroidery Book.* New York: Scribner's, 1973. (374 pp.) Includes counted-thread embroidery, couching, Holbein work, drawn-thread embroidery, shadow work, stumpwork, and canvas embroidery. Historical background of various embroidery techniques.

Wilson, Jean. *Weaving is Creative—The Weaver-Controlled Weaves.* New York: Van Nostrand Reinhold, 1972. (268 pp.) Includes twining, chaining, soumak, inlay, leno, gauze, tapestry, knotting, finishings, and joinings.

Index

The close relationship between weaving and needlework encourages more and more fiber workers to combine these two techniques. Until now, however, no book existed to guide experimenters in the methods.

EMBROIDERING WITH THE LOOM: CREATIVE COMBINATIONS OF WEAVING AND STITCHERY integrates many weaving and needlework techniques to achieve unique effects, as well as to save time and effort. The book divides these techniques into three categories: embroidery over specially woven background fabrics, embroidery over empty warp or weft threads, and embroidery stitches partially produced by means of the loom. The last category makes use of the mechanical action of the loom to speed up some of the repetitive aspects of counted-thread embroidery.

An acquaintance with weaving, without prior experience with embroidery, fulfills all the background requirements for using the techniques described. A novice handweaver familiar with the four-harness loom can carry out every operation discussed in the book. Anyone who has been introduced to a simple frame loom can work almost half of the techniques, including all those that employ embroidery stitches over empty warp threads. Embroiderers with no prior experience in weaving may well be inspired to acquire the working knowledge necessary to try for themselves.

Although the techniques involved are quite simple, the interaction of weaving and embroidery can produce seemingly complex results. Certain effects are impossible to execute with either technique alone.

The exciting results have applications in both traditional and contemporary projects. Designs for clothing, accessories, furnishings, and fiber-art pieces are included, as are descriptions of all tools and materials necessary. Naturally, fiber workers can adapt any of the techniques discussed to their particular interests, and can then go on to invent original combinations and applications.